Custer's Last Stand

written by **Joeming Dunn**
illustrated by **Ben Dunn**

magic
wagon

visit us at
www.abdopublishing.com

Published by Magic Wagon, a division of the ABDO Publishing Group, 8000 West 78th Street, Edina, Minnesota 55439. Copyright © 2009 by Abdo Consulting Group, Inc. International copyrights reserved in all countries. All rights reserved. No part of this book may be reproduced in any form without written permission from the publisher.
Graphic Planet™ is a trademark and logo of Magic Wagon.

Printed in the United States.

Written by Joeming Dunn
Illustrated by Ben Dunn
Colored by Robby Bevard
Lettered by Joeming Dunn
Edited by Stephanie Hedlund and Rochelle Baltzer
Interior layout and design by Antarctic Press
Cover art by Ben Dunn
Cover design by Neil Klinepier

Library of Congress Cataloging-in-Publication Data

Dunn, Joeming W.
   Custer's last stand / written by Joeming Dunn ; illustrated by Ben Dunn.
     p. cm. -- (Graphic history)
   Includes bibliographic references and index.
   ISBN 978-1-60270-181-6
   1. Little Bighorn, Battle of the, Mont., 1876--Juvenile literature. 2. Custer, George A. (George Armstrong), 1839-1876--Juvenile literature. I. Dunn, Ben. II. Title.

E83.876.D86 2008
973.8'2--dc22

                                           2007051654

TABLE of CONTENTS

Timeline..4

Chapter 1
Louisiana Purchase...............................6

Chapter 2
The Second Fort Laramie Treaty........10

Chapter 3
The Yellowstone Expedition..............14

Chapter 4
Battle of Little Bighorn.....................18

Chapter 5
Custer's Last Stand..........................24

Map of Little Bighorn........................30

Glossary..31

Web Sites...31

Index...32

Timeline

1783 - The Treaty of Paris ended the Revolutionary War.

1800 - Thomas Jefferson was elected the third president of the United States of America.

1803 - The Louisiana Purchase expanded the United States. The Lewis and Clark Expedition explored the area.

1840s - The gold rush brought settlers west; they began taking over Native American lands.

1868 - The Second Fort Laramie Treaty required the U.S. government to protect Lakota lands from white settlers.

1874 - George Armstrong Custer announced the discovery of gold in the Black Hills. This set off a rush of settlers into this most sacred part of Lakota territory.

1876 - On June 25, George Armstrong Custer discovered Sitting Bull's encampment on the Little Bighorn River. Hundreds of Lakota warriors overwhelmed his troops in a battle later called Custer's Last Stand. News of the massacre shocked the nation.

1877 - Congress voted to repeal the 1868 Second Fort Laramie Treaty. It took back the Black Hills, along with 40 million more acres of Lakota land.

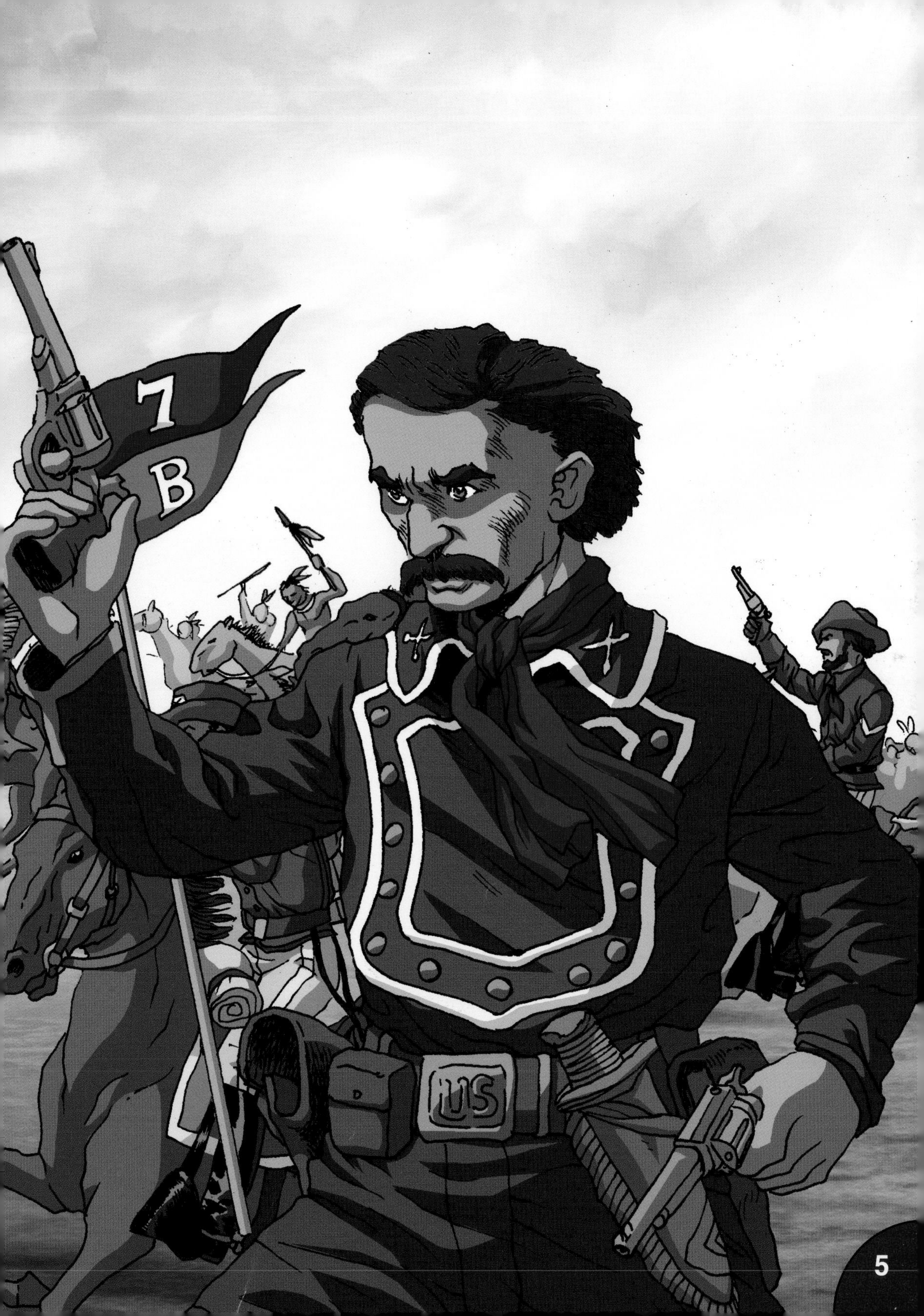
7
B
US

Chapter 1 Louisiana Purchase

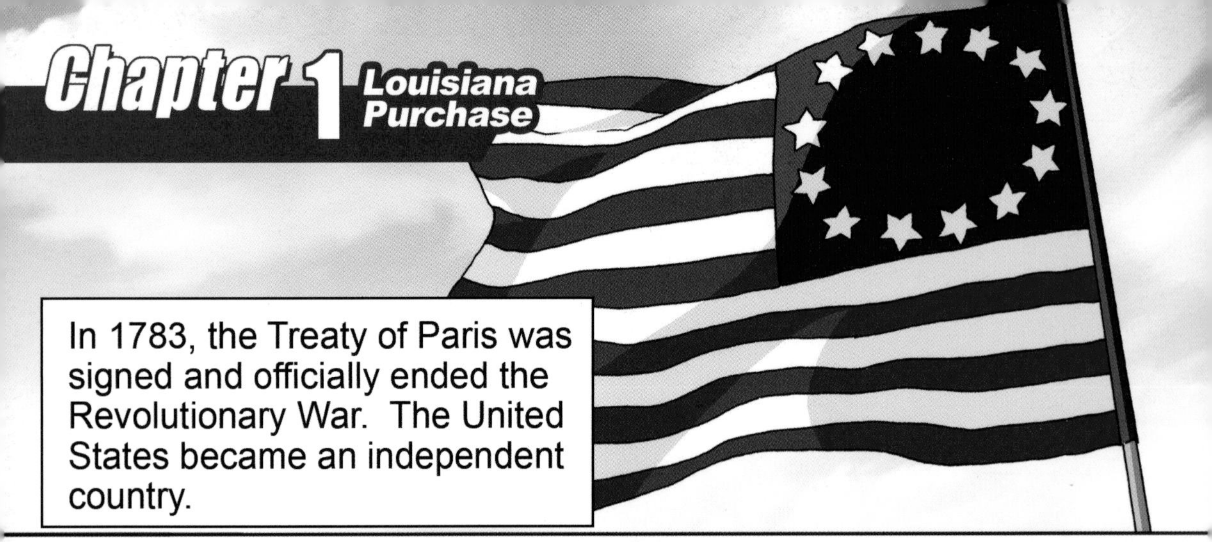
In 1783, the Treaty of Paris was signed and officially ended the Revolutionary War. The United States became an independent country.

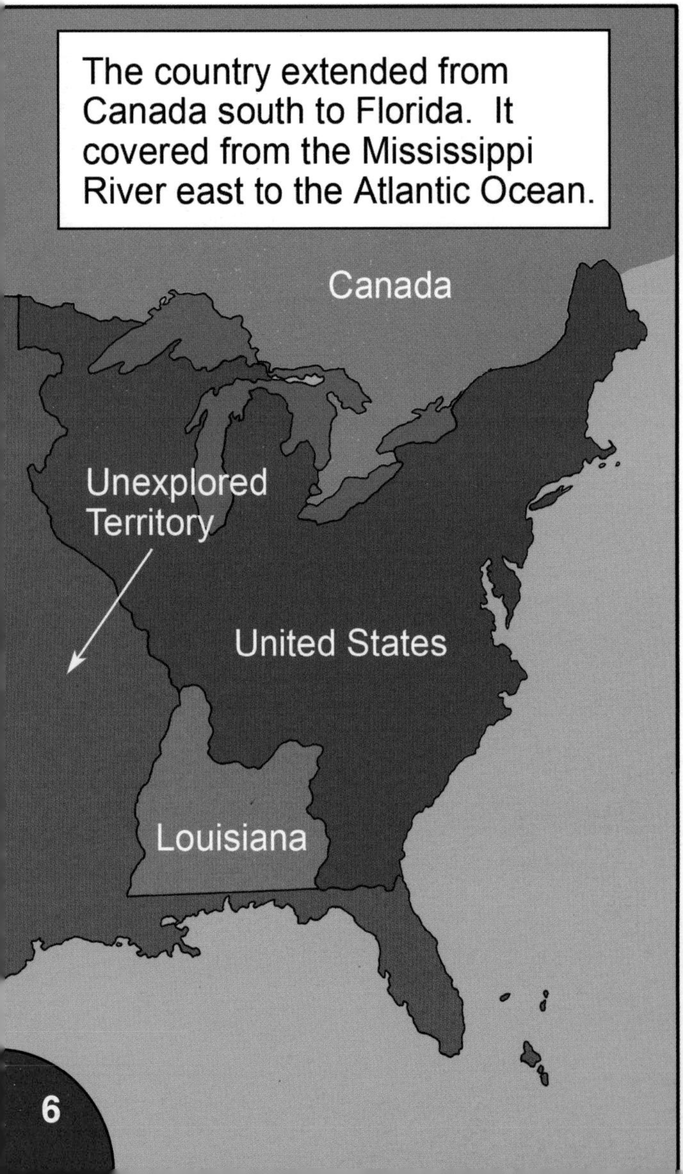
The country extended from Canada south to Florida. It covered from the Mississippi River east to the Atlantic Ocean.
Canada
Unexplored Territory
United States
Louisiana

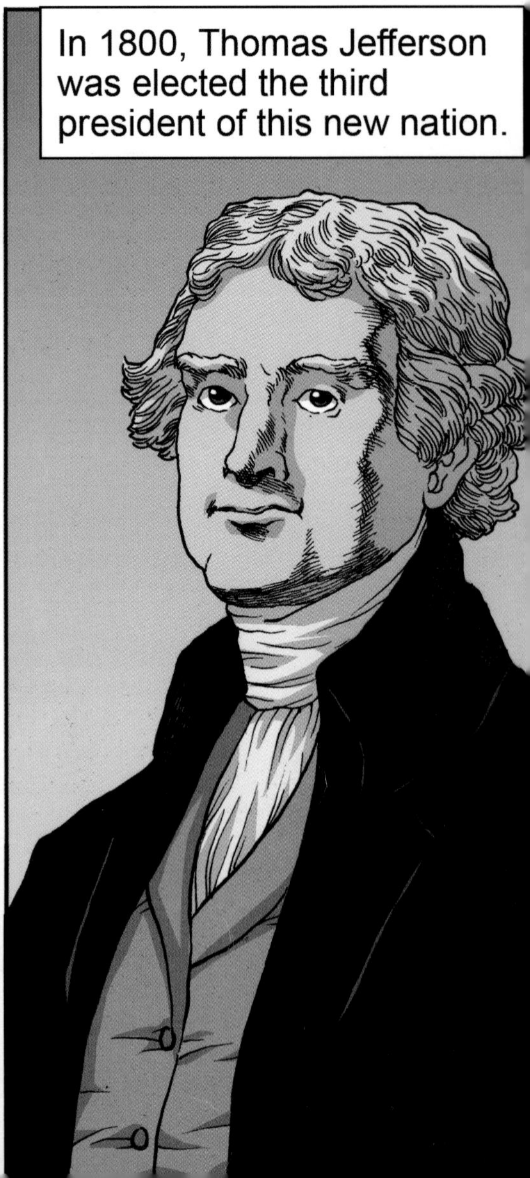
In 1800, Thomas Jefferson was elected the third president of this new nation.

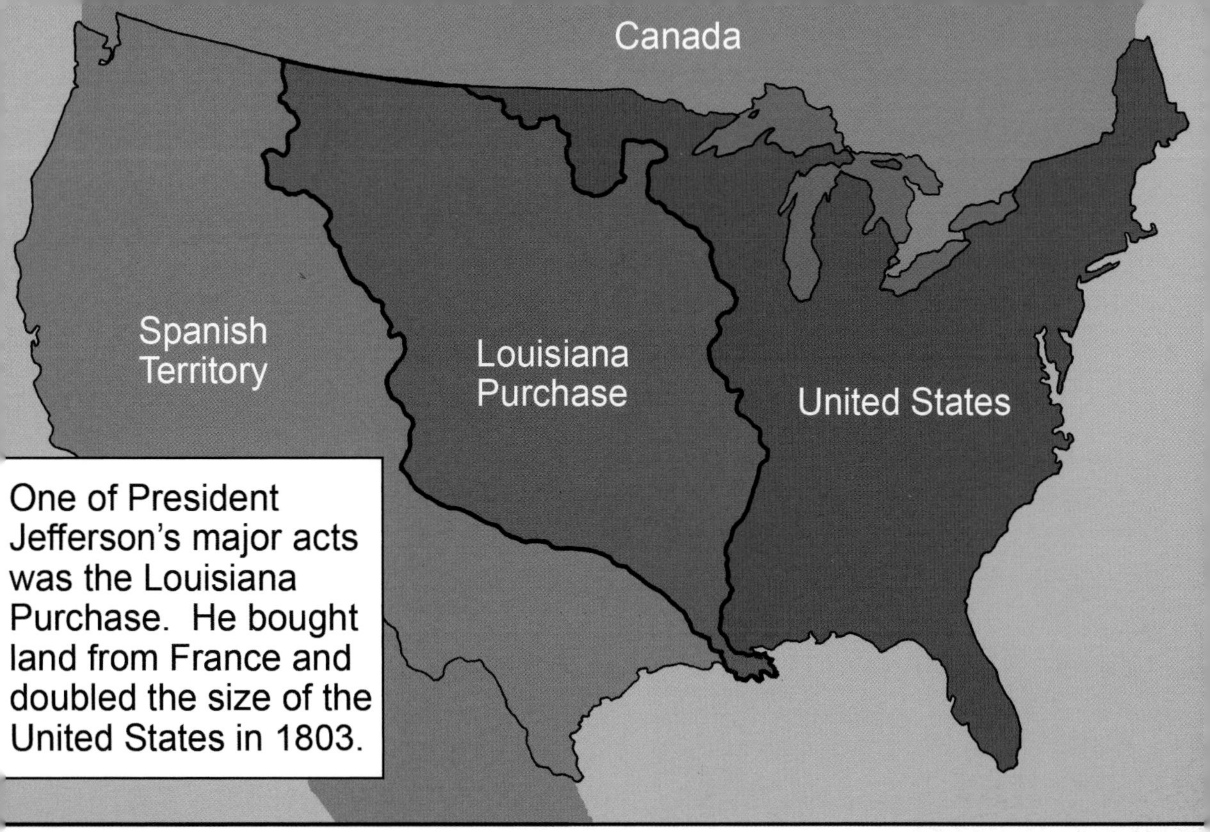
Canada
Spanish Territory
Louisiana Purchase
United States
One of President Jefferson's major acts was the Louisiana Purchase. He bought land from France and doubled the size of the United States in 1803.

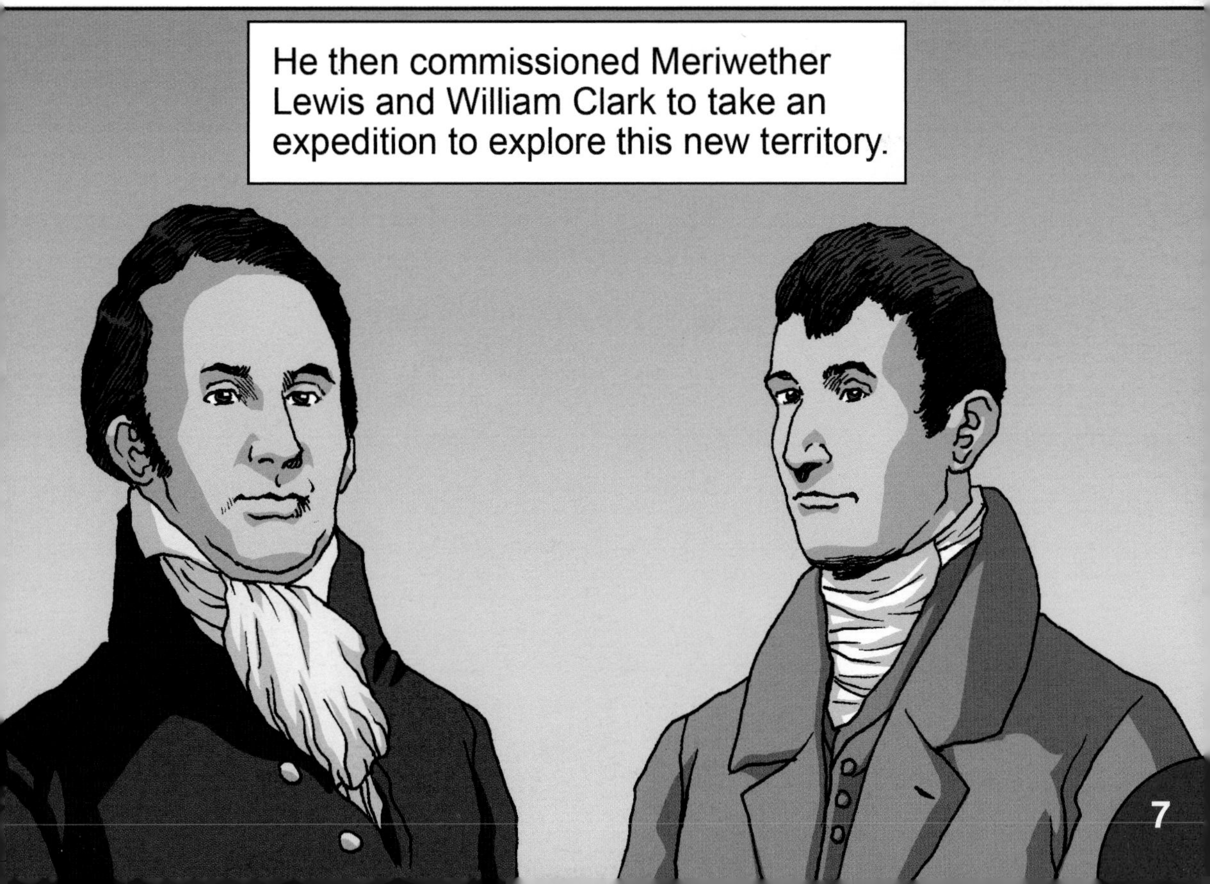
He then commissioned Meriwether Lewis and William Clark to take an expedition to explore this new territory.

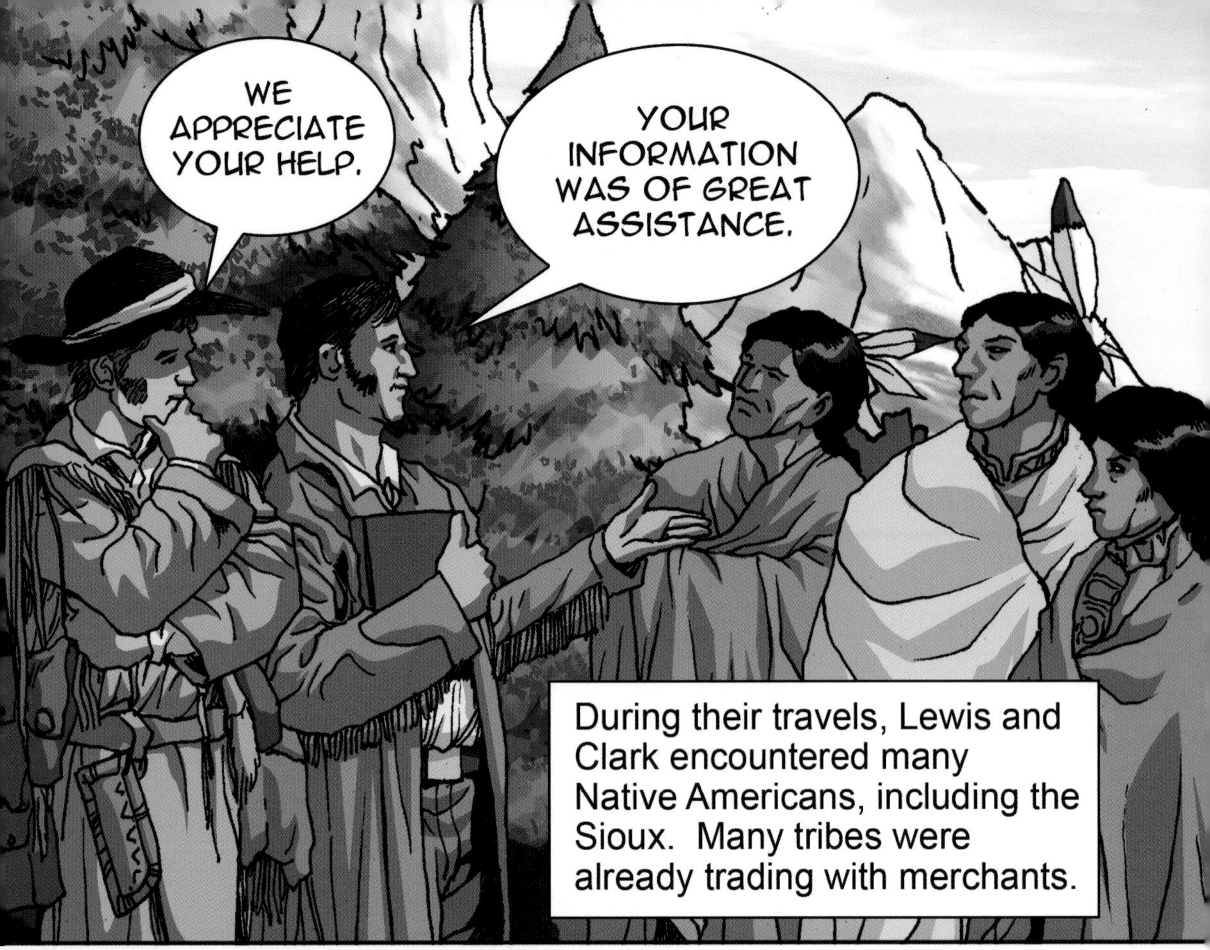
WE APPRECIATE YOUR HELP.
YOUR INFORMATION WAS OF GREAT ASSISTANCE.
During their travels, Lewis and Clark encountered many Native Americans, including the Sioux. Many tribes were already trading with merchants.

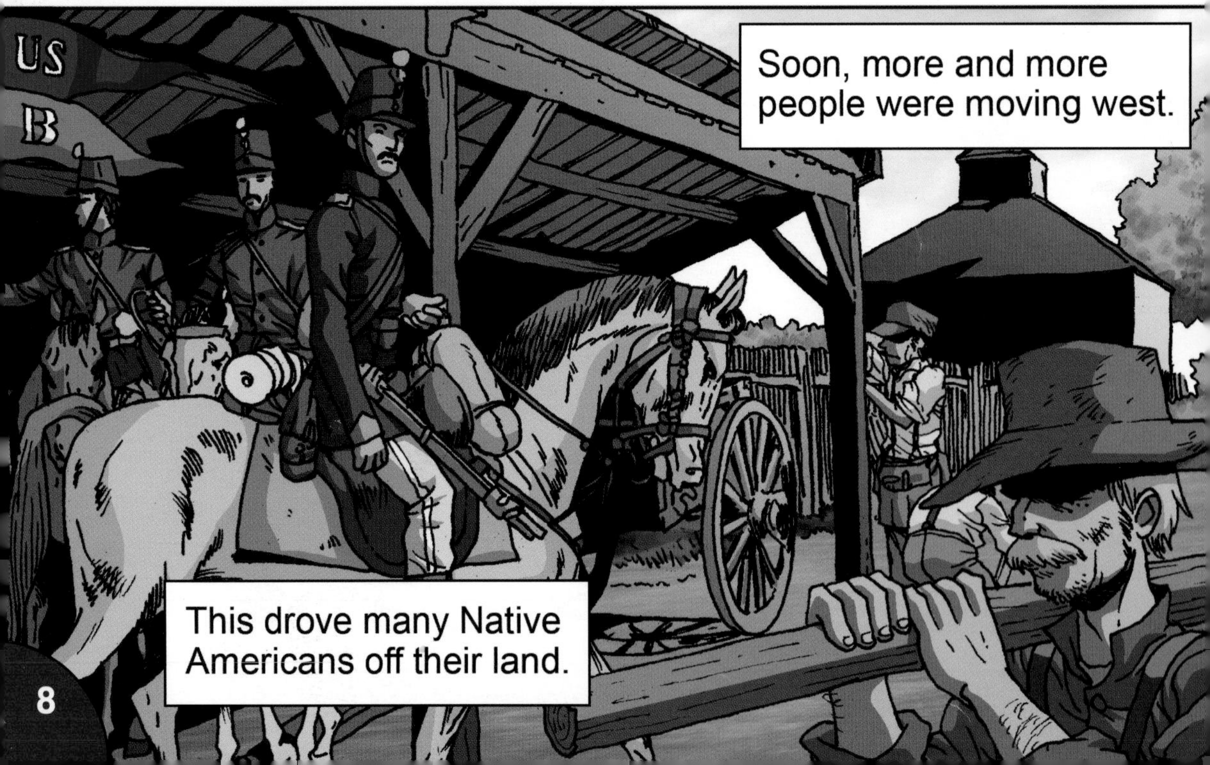
US
B
Soon, more and more people were moving west.
This drove many Native Americans off their land.

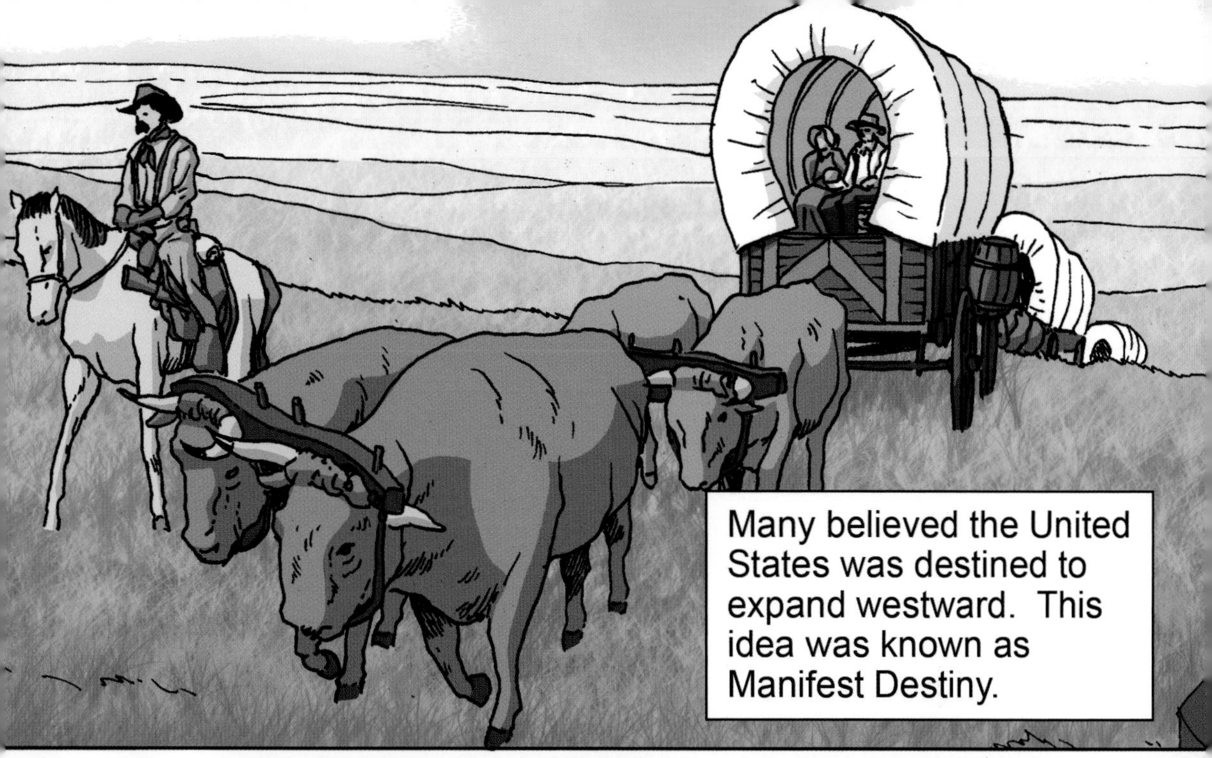
Many believed the United States was destined to expand westward. This idea was known as Manifest Destiny.

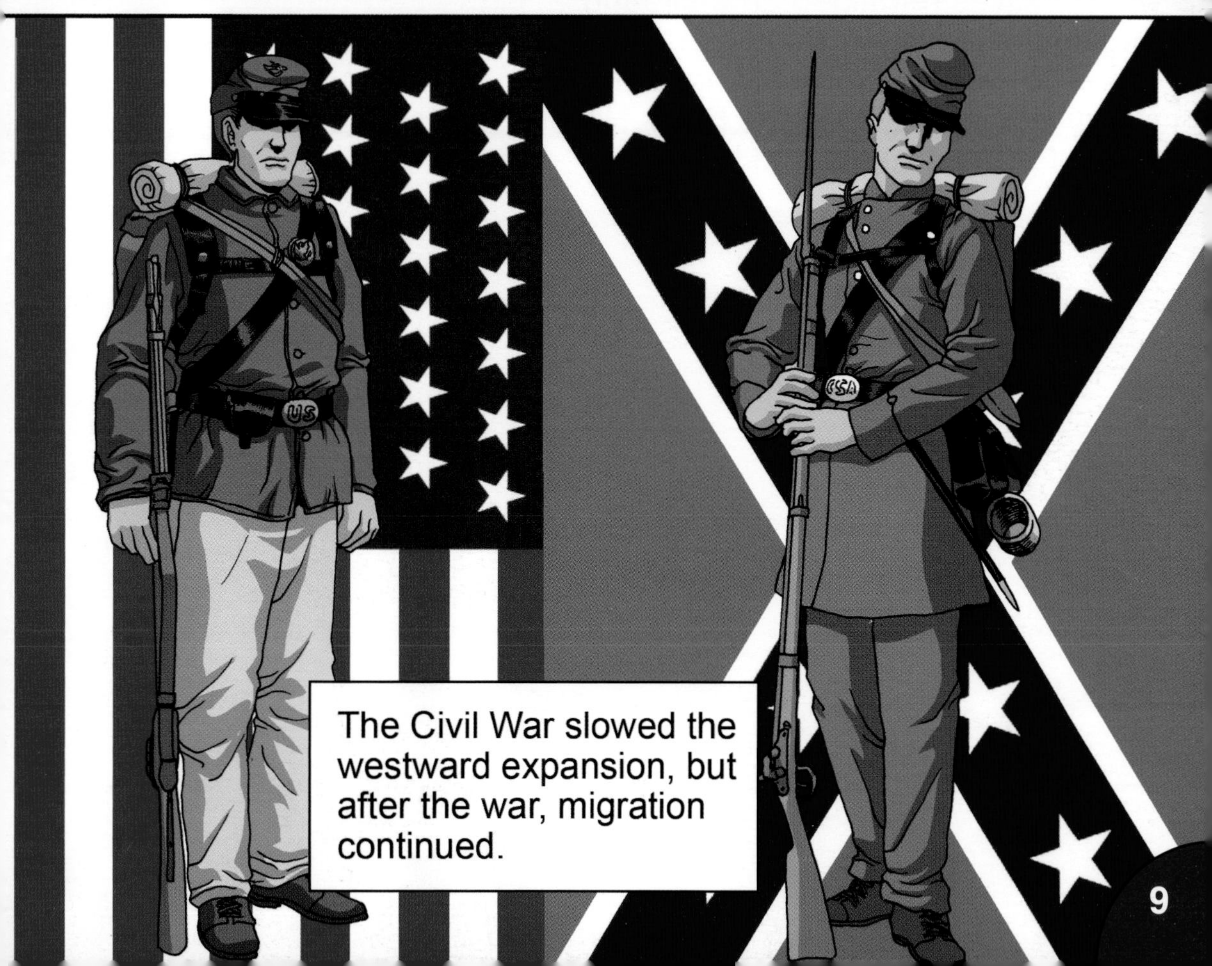
US
CSA
The Civil War slowed the westward expansion, but after the war, migration continued.

Chapter 2 The Second Fort Laramie Treaty

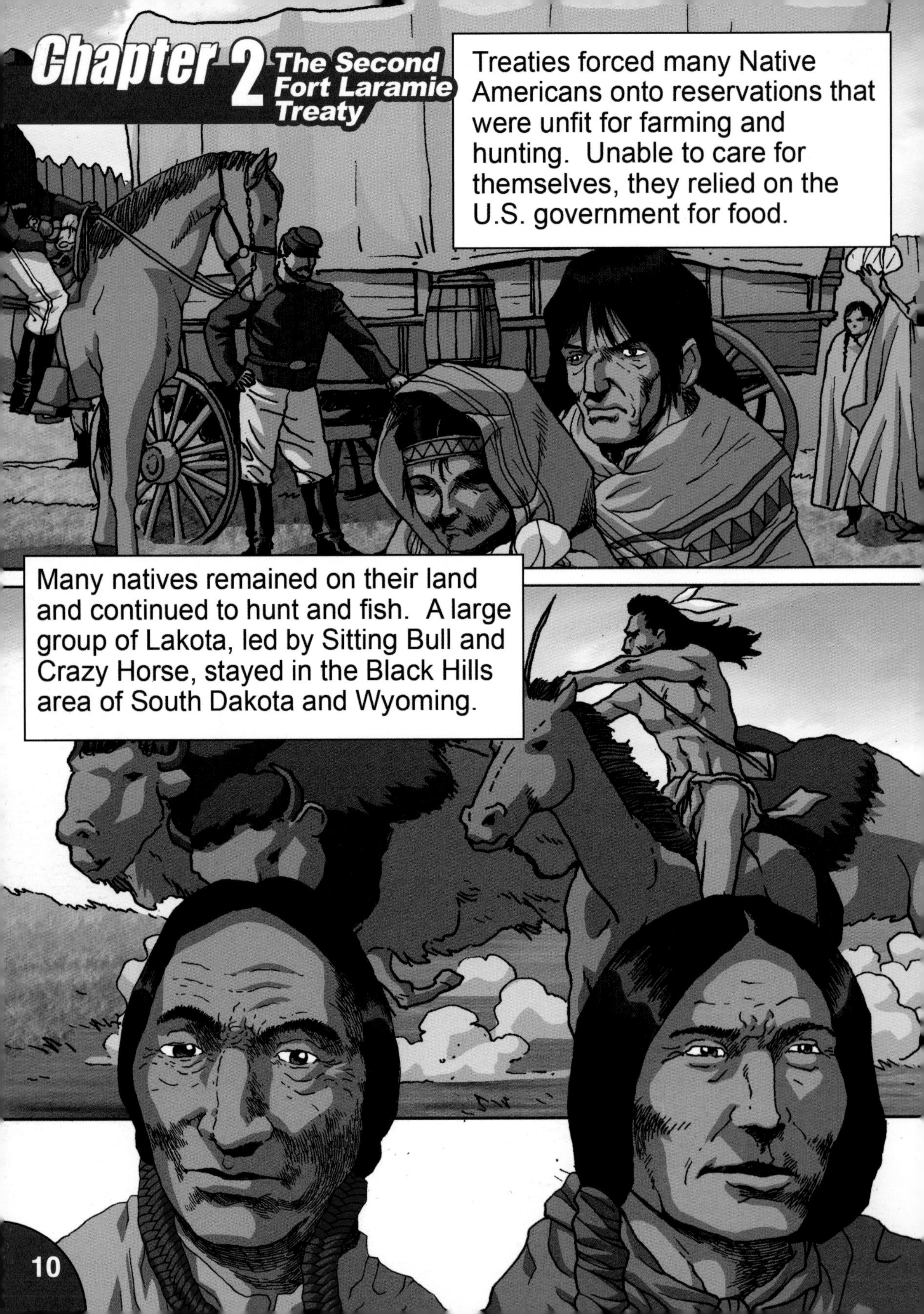
Treaties forced many Native Americans onto reservations that were unfit for farming and hunting. Unable to care for themselves, they relied on the U.S. government for food.
Many natives remained on their land and continued to hunt and fish. A large group of Lakota, led by Sitting Bull and Crazy Horse, stayed in the Black Hills area of South Dakota and Wyoming.

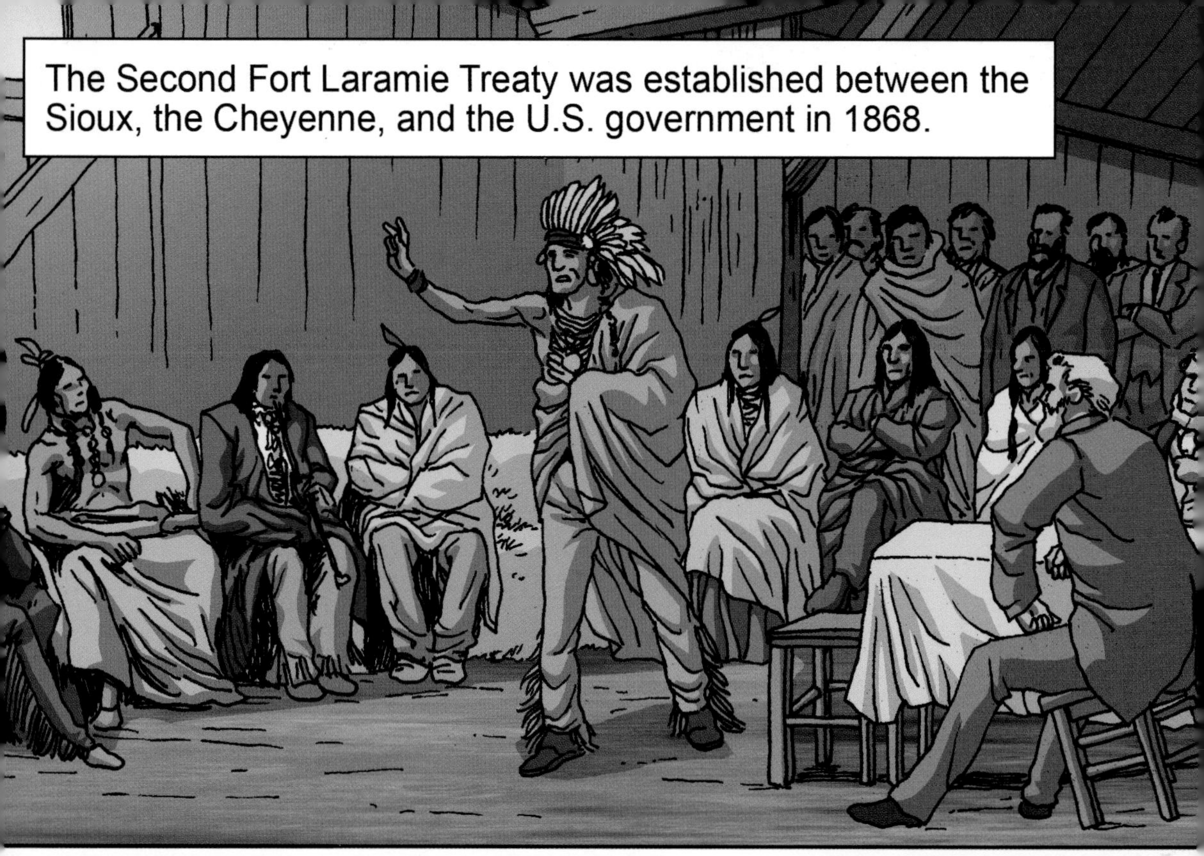
The Second Fort Laramie Treaty was established between the Sioux, the Cheyenne, and the U.S. government in 1868.

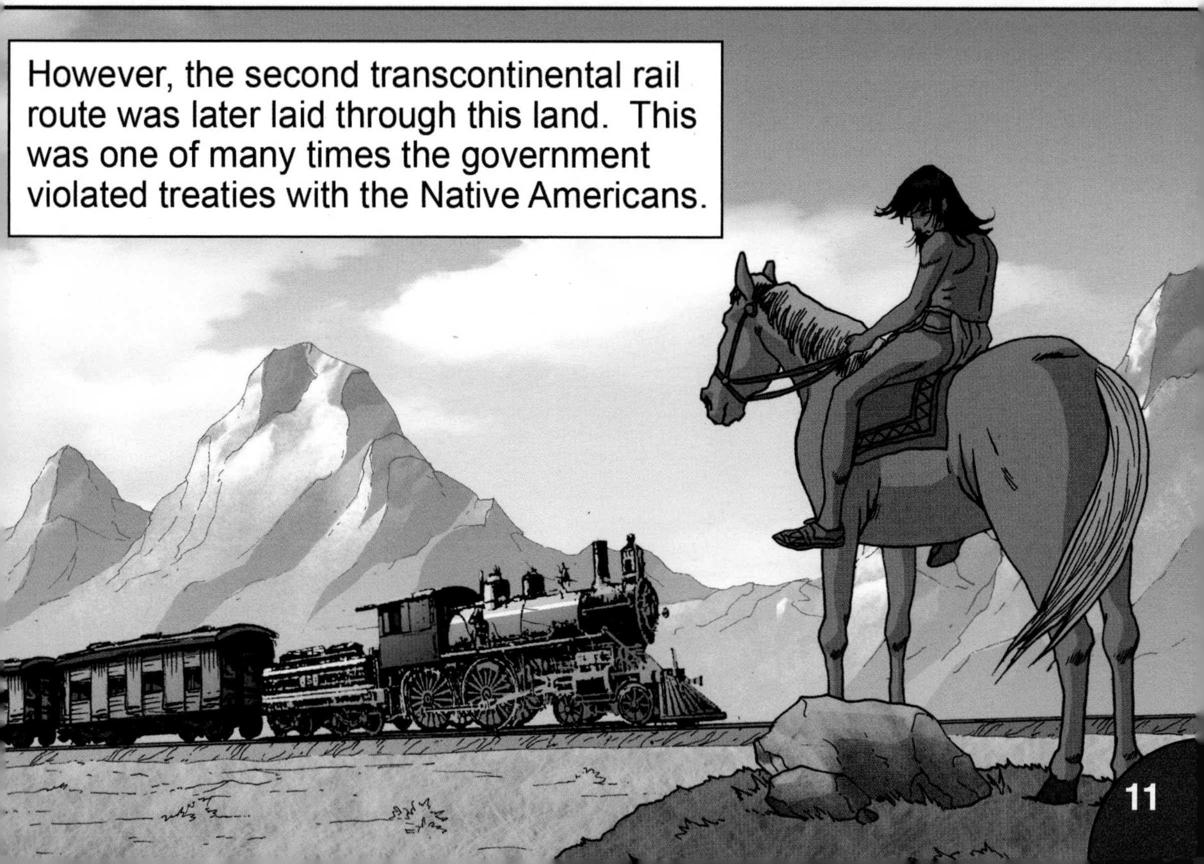
However, the second transcontinental rail route was later laid through this land. This was one of many times the government violated treaties with the Native Americans.

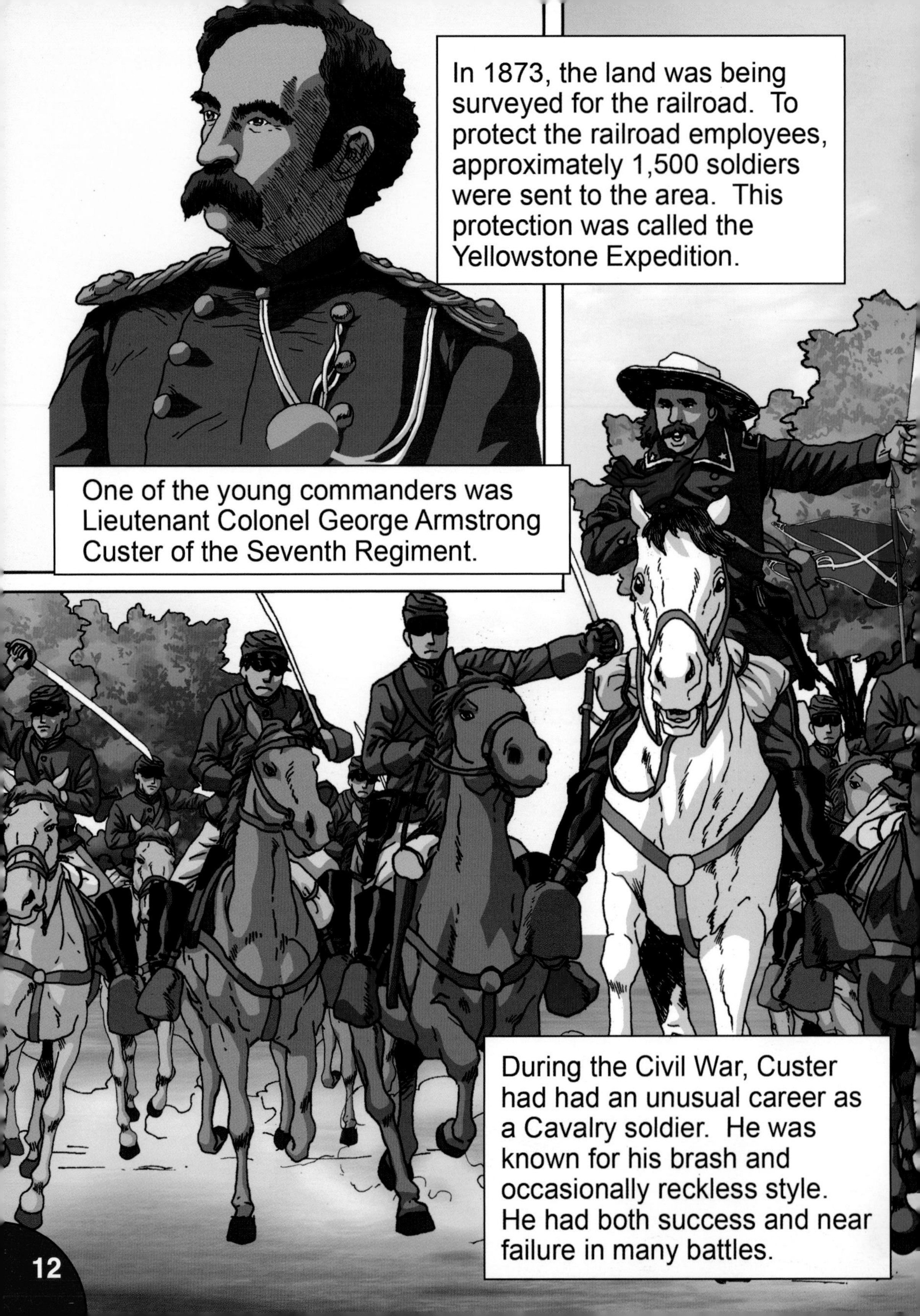
In 1873, the land was being surveyed for the railroad. To protect the railroad employees, approximately 1,500 soldiers were sent to the area. This protection was called the Yellowstone Expedition.
One of the young commanders was Lieutenant Colonel George Armstrong Custer of the Seventh Regiment.
During the Civil War, Custer had had an unusual career as a Cavalry soldier. He was known for his brash and occasionally reckless style. He had both success and near failure in many battles.

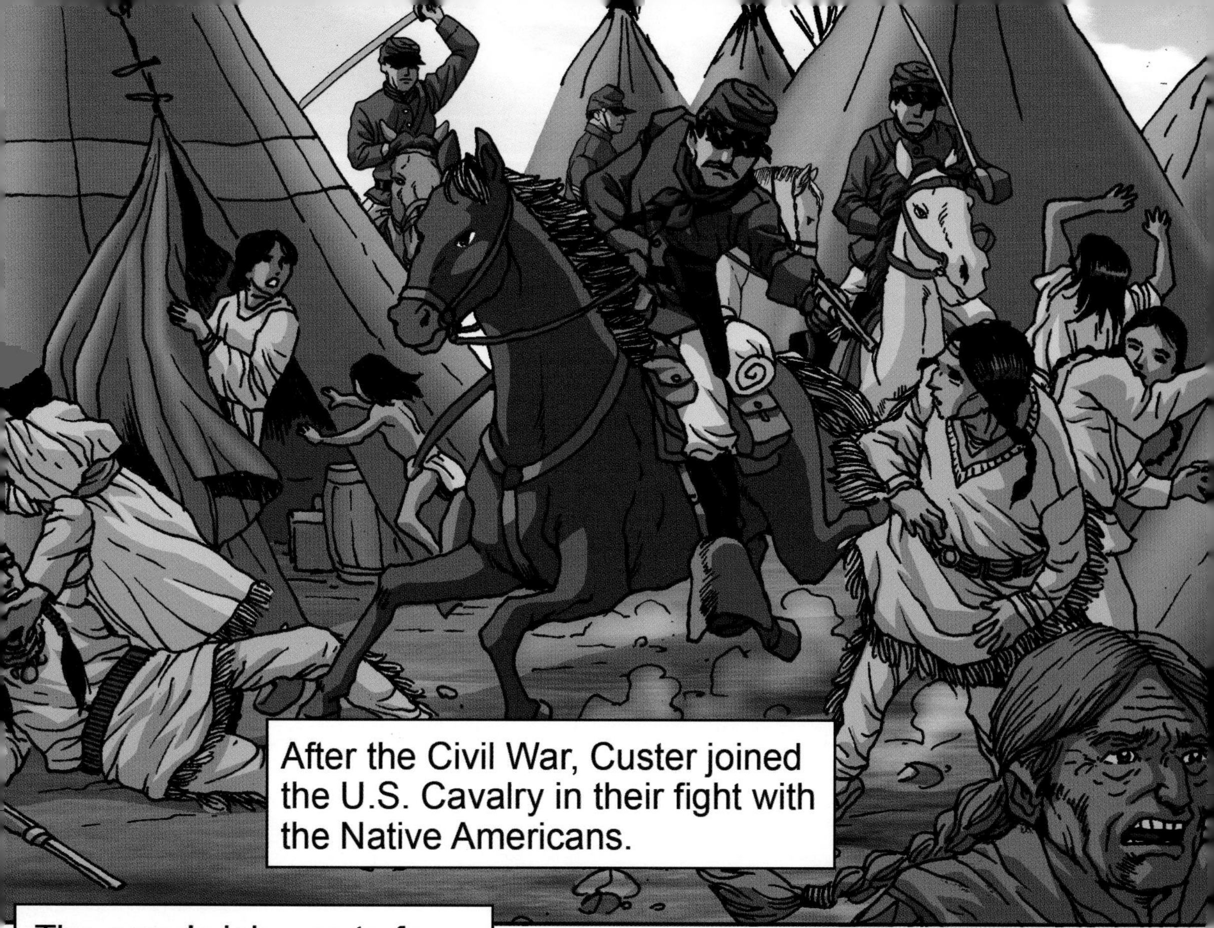
After the Civil War, Custer joined the U.S. Cavalry in their fight with the Native Americans.

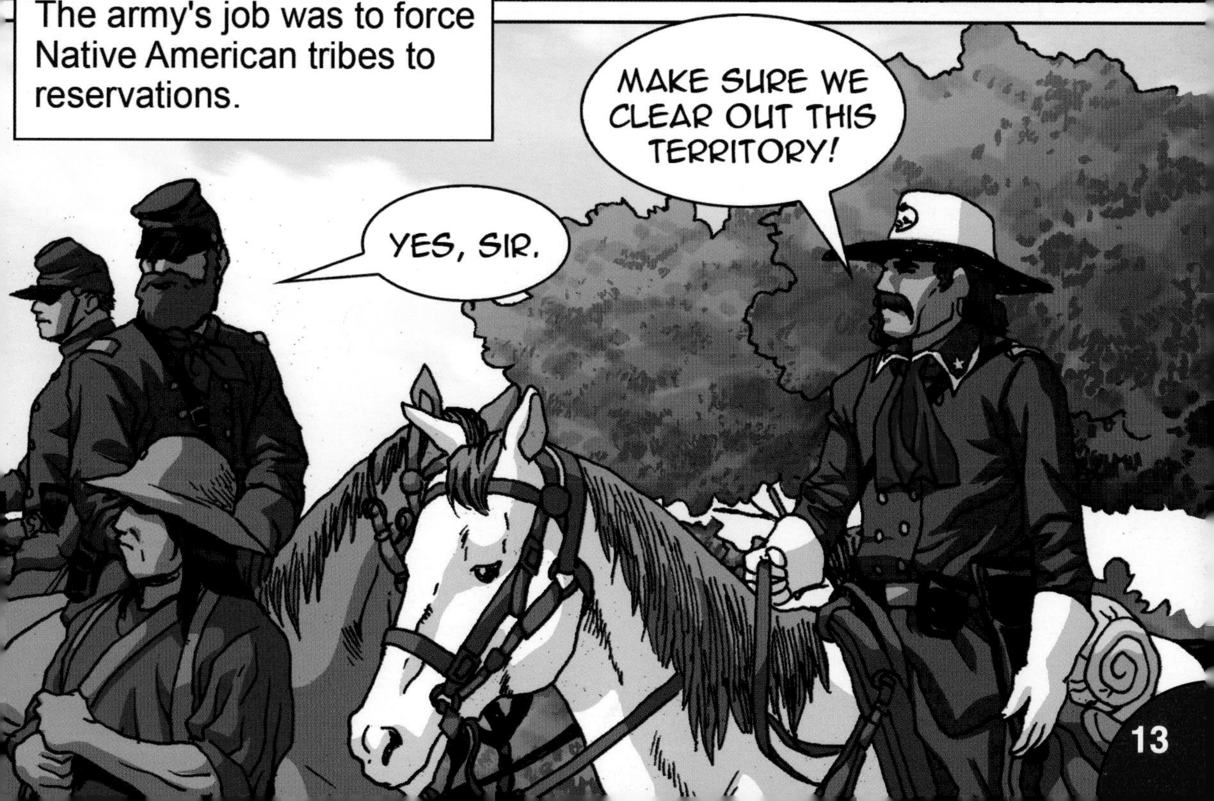
The army's job was to force Native American tribes to reservations.
MAKE SURE WE CLEAR OUT THIS TERRITORY!
YES, SIR.

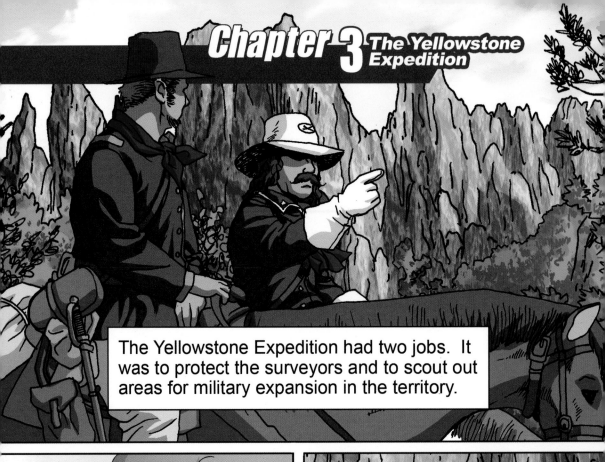

Chapter 3 The Yellowstone Expedition
The Yellowstone Expedition had two jobs. It was to protect the surveyors and to scout out areas for military expansion in the territory.
Unfortunately, much of the area was considered sacred to the Lakota and the Cheyenne.
The expedition also confirmed there was gold in the hills.

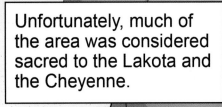

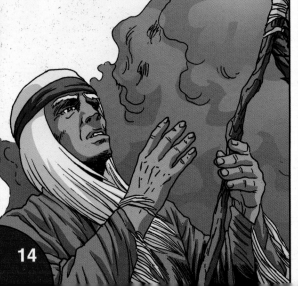

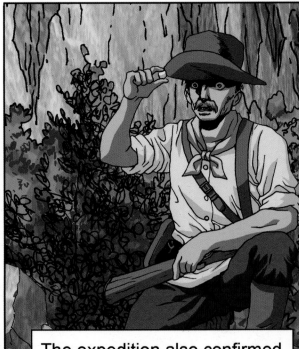

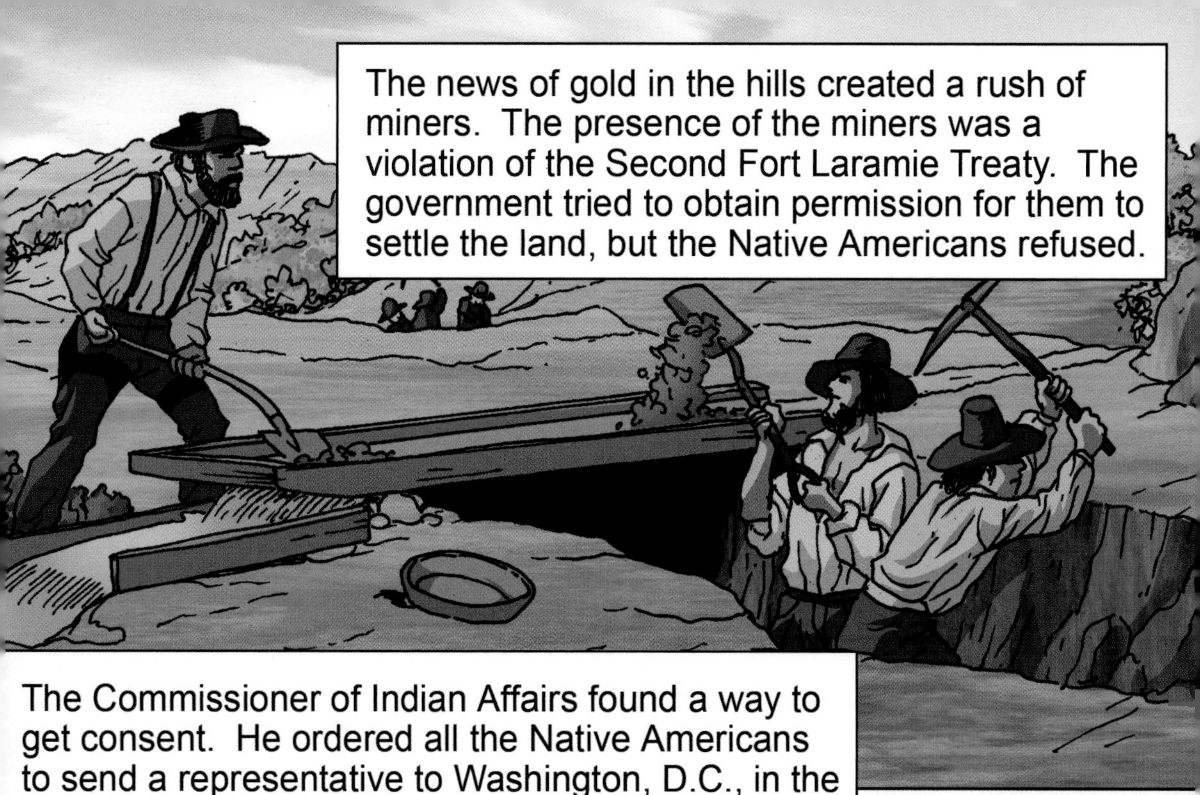
The news of gold in the hills created a rush of miners. The presence of the miners was a violation of the Second Fort Laramie Treaty. The government tried to obtain permission for them to settle the land, but the Native Americans refused.

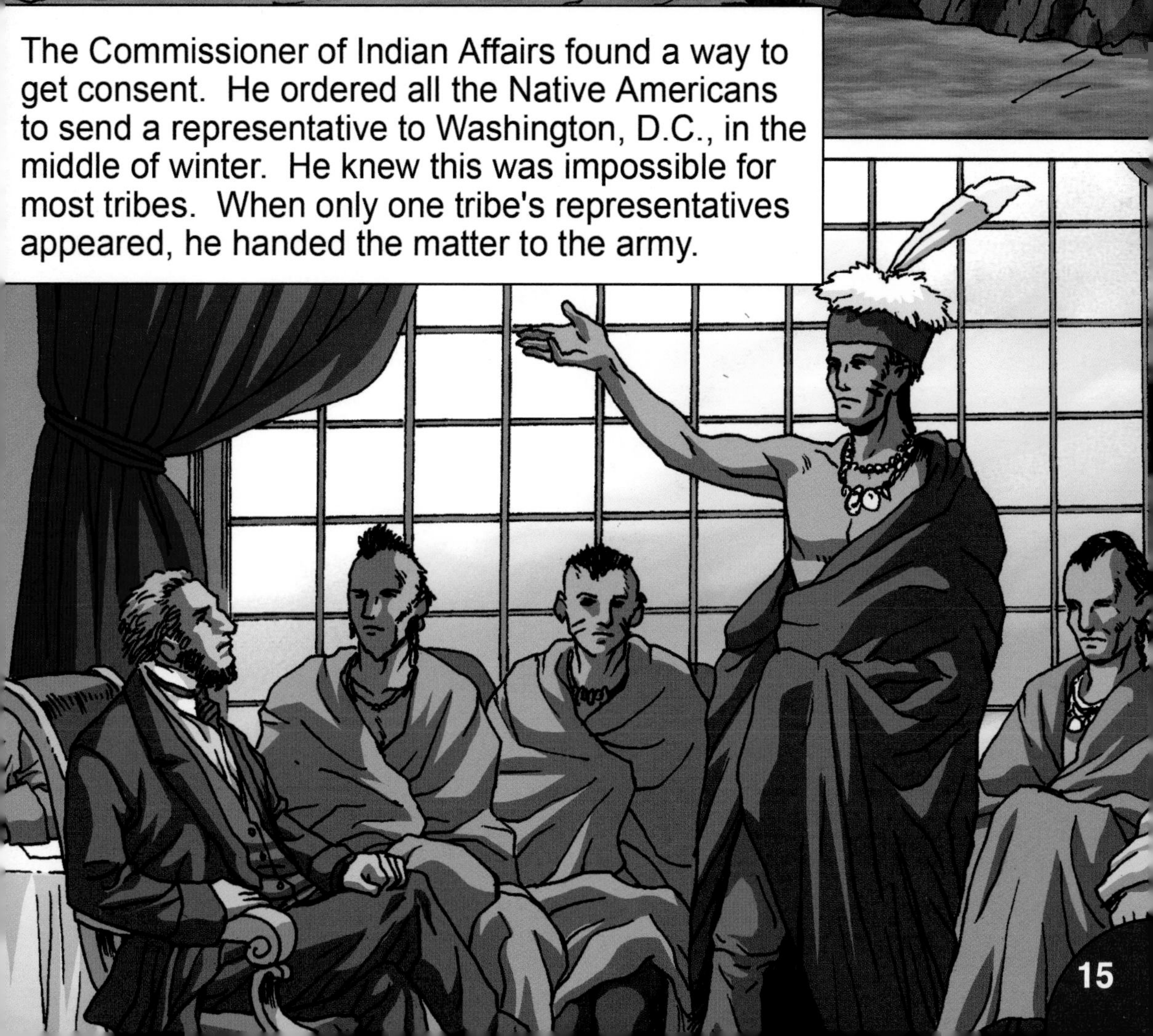
The Commissioner of Indian Affairs found a way to get consent. He ordered all the Native Americans to send a representative to Washington, D.C., in the middle of winter. He knew this was impossible for most tribes. When only one tribe's representatives appeared, he handed the matter to the army.

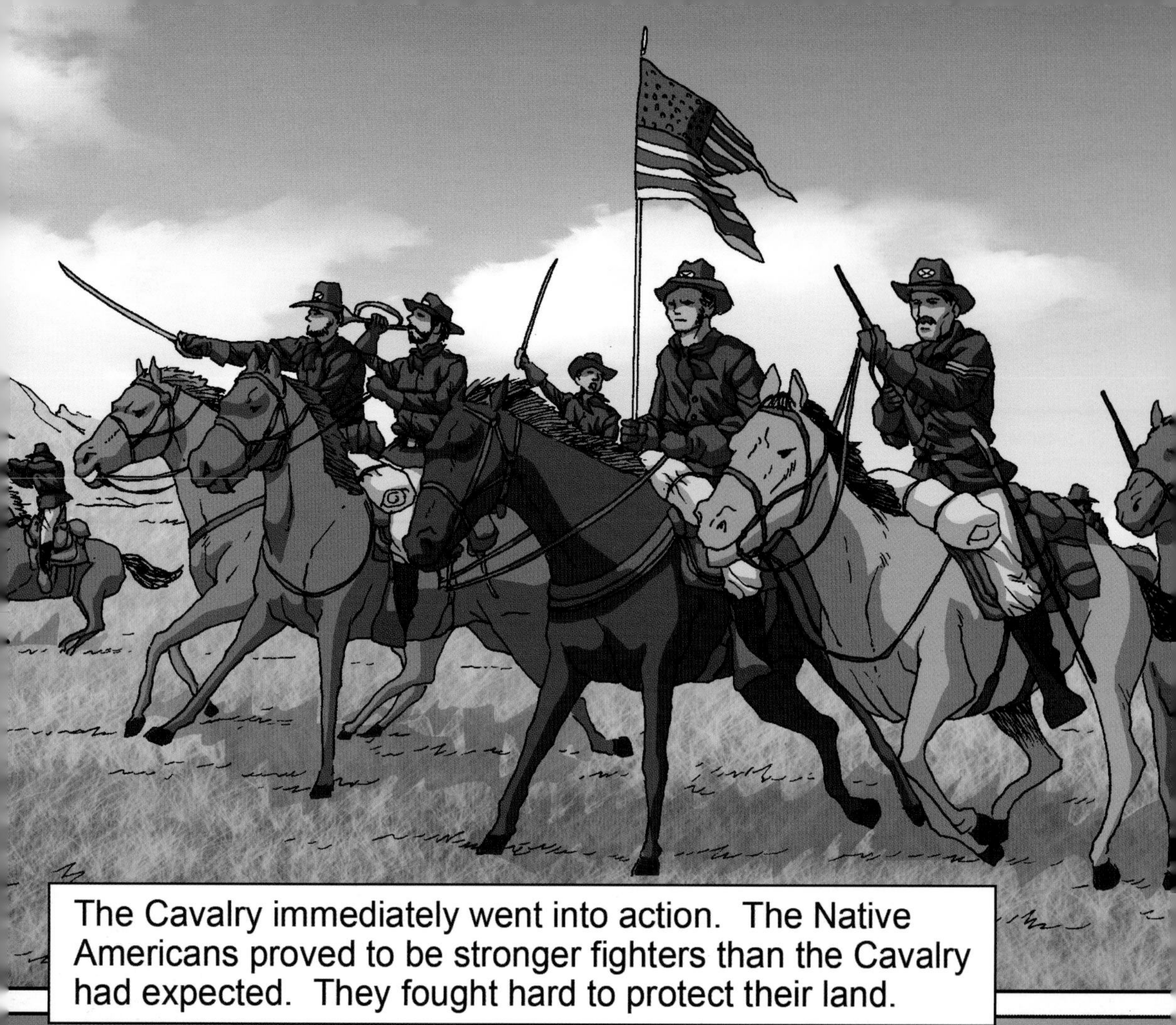
The Cavalry immediately went into action. The Native Americans proved to be stronger fighters than the Cavalry had expected. They fought hard to protect their land.

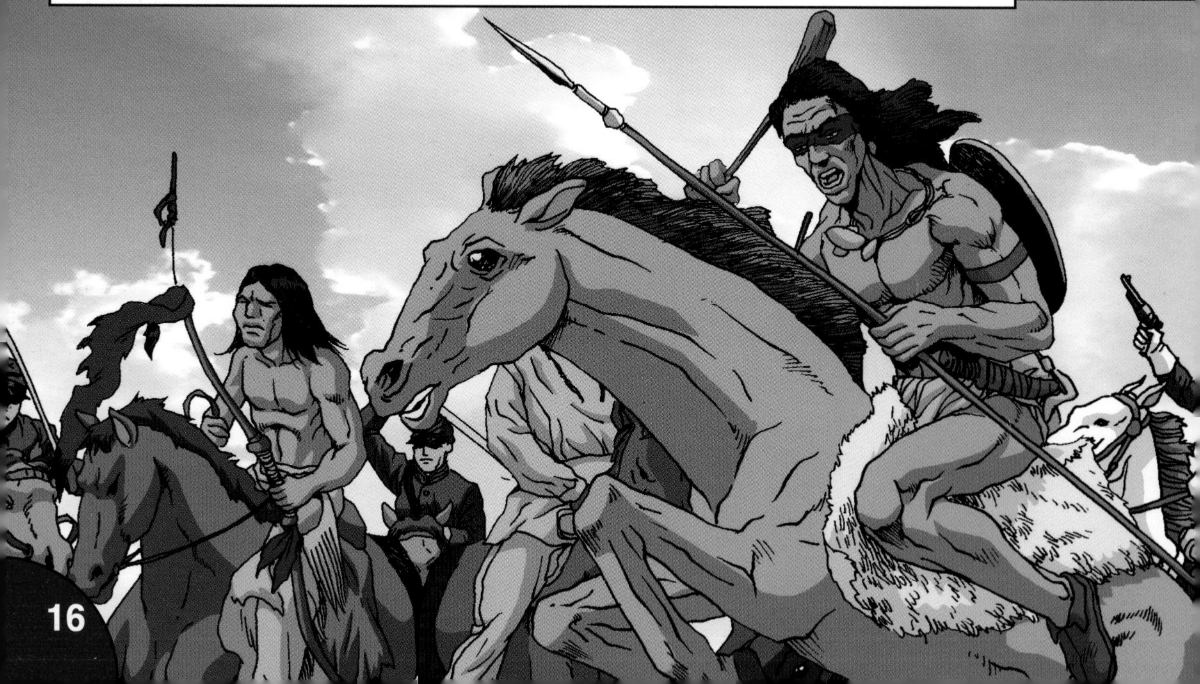

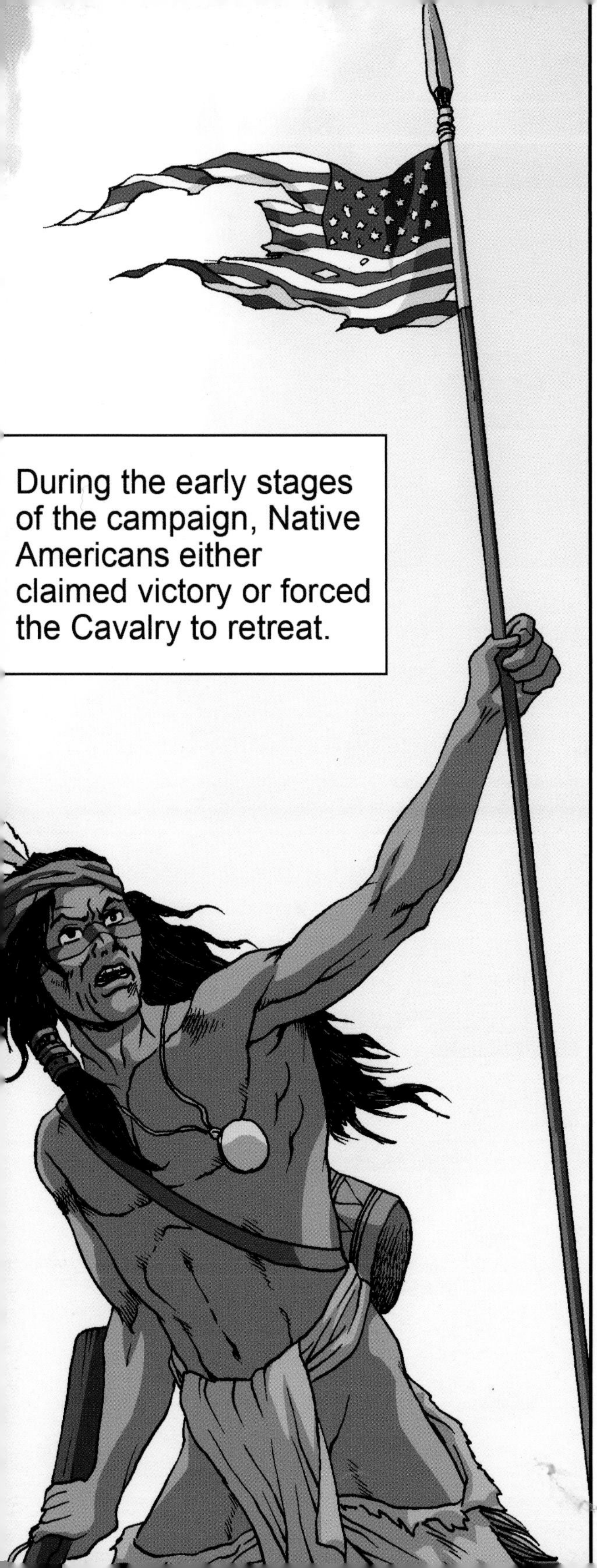
During the early stages of the campaign, Native Americans either claimed victory or forced the Cavalry to retreat.

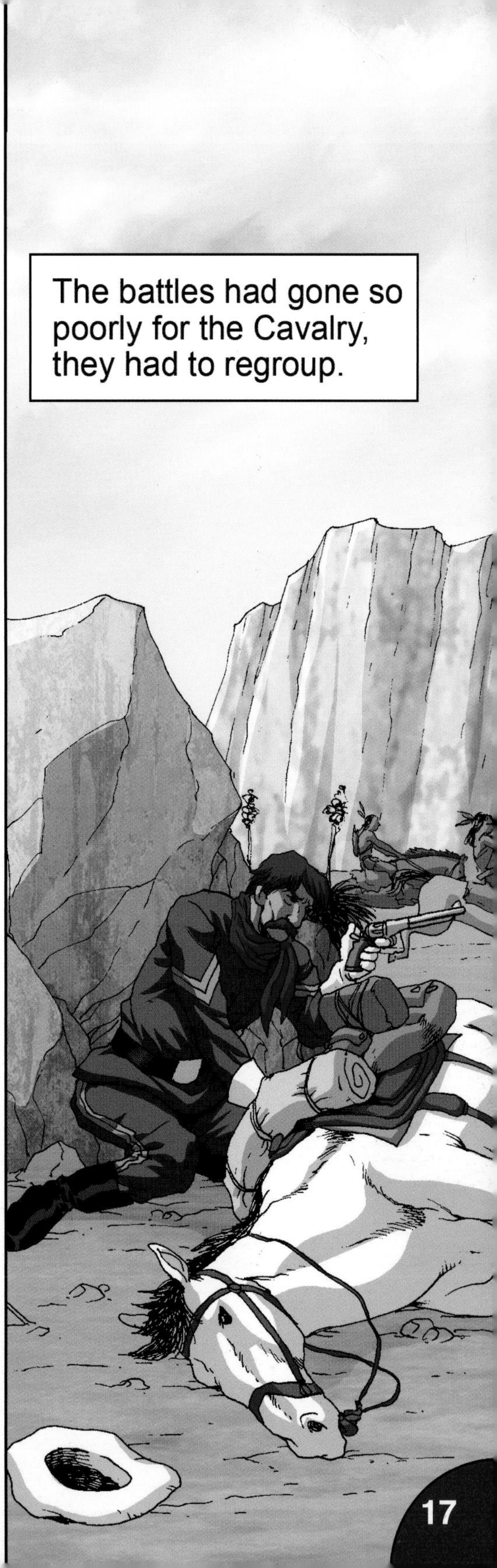
The battles had gone so poorly for the Cavalry, they had to regroup.

Chapter 4
Battle of Little Bighorn

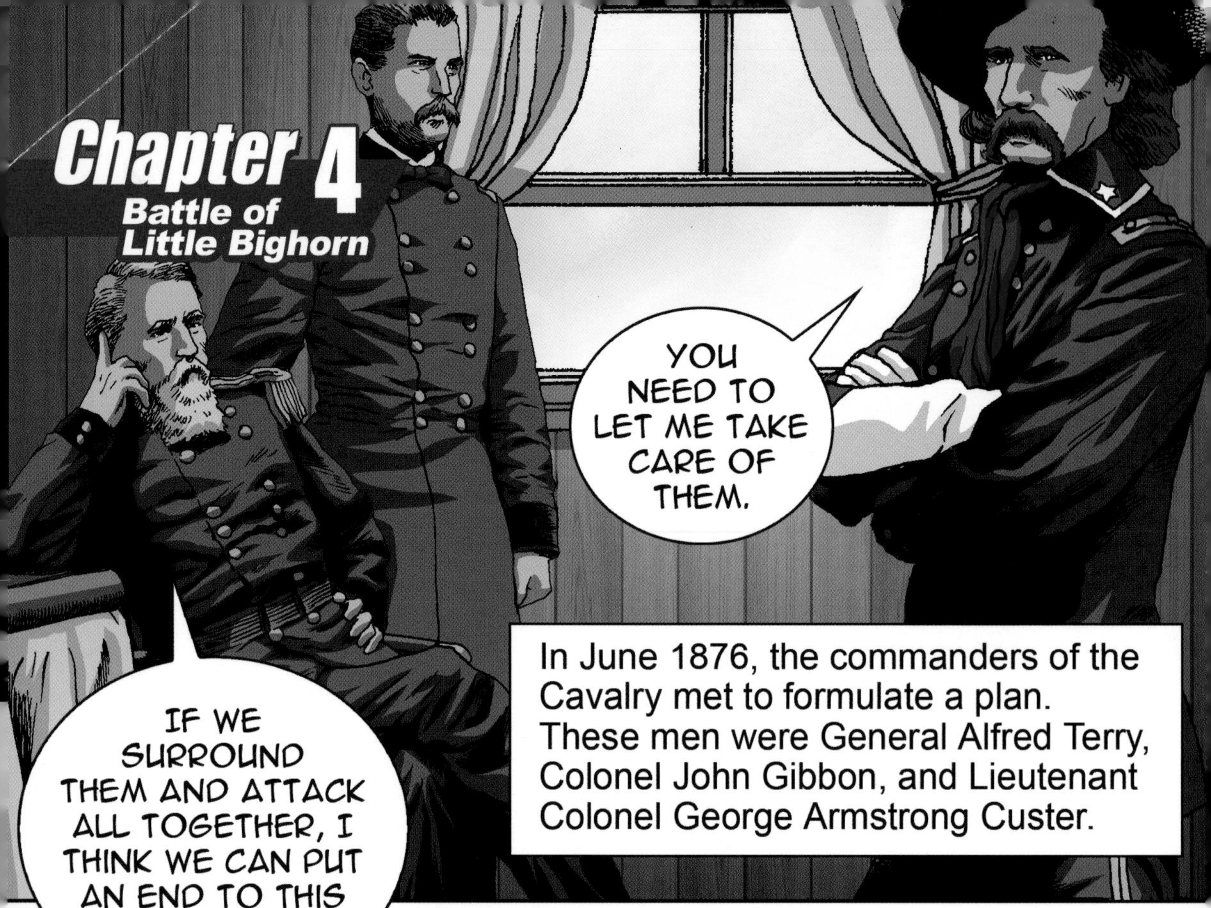

In June 1876, the commanders of the Cavalry met to formulate a plan. These men were General Alfred Terry, Colonel John Gibbon, and Lieutenant Colonel George Armstrong Custer.
IF WE SURROUND THEM AND ATTACK ALL TOGETHER, I THINK WE CAN PUT AN END TO THIS RESISTANCE.
YOU NEED TO LET ME TAKE CARE OF THEM.

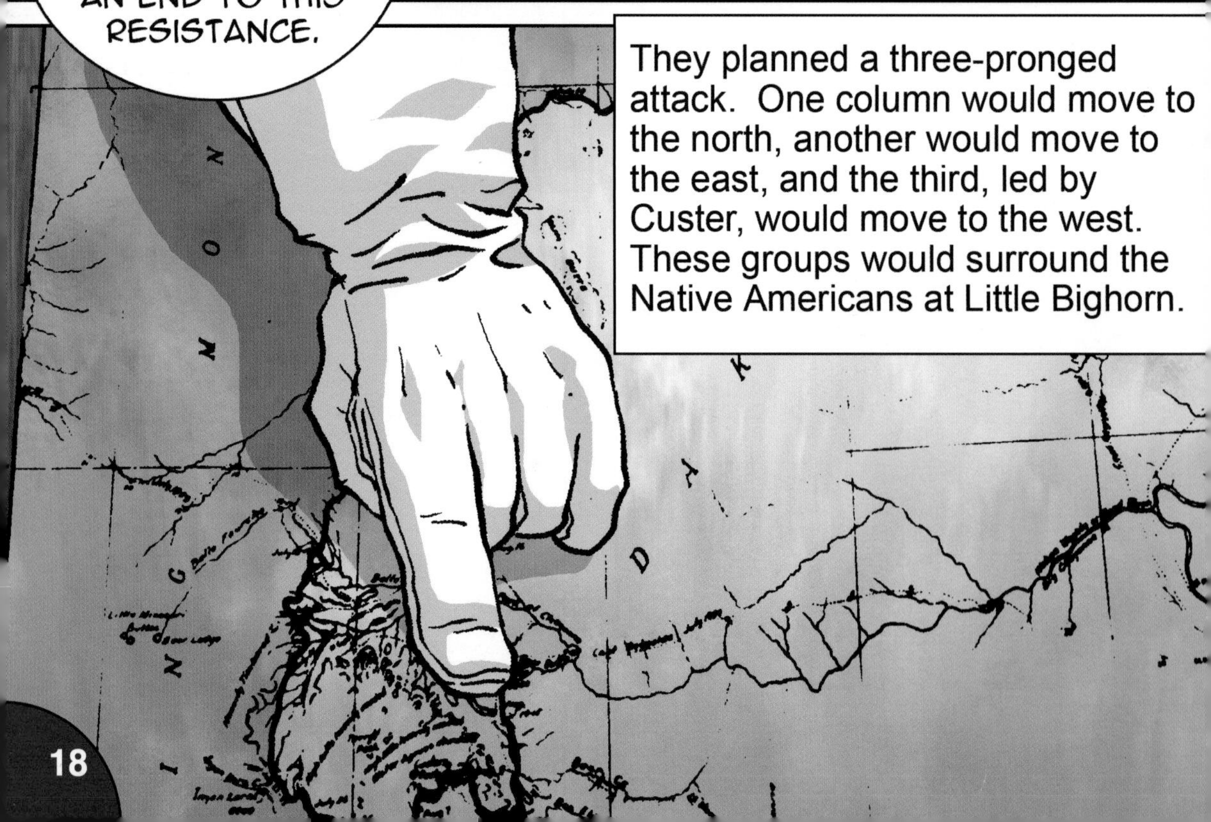

They planned a three-pronged attack. One column would move to the north, another would move to the east, and the third, led by Custer, would move to the west. These groups would surround the Native Americans at Little Bighorn.

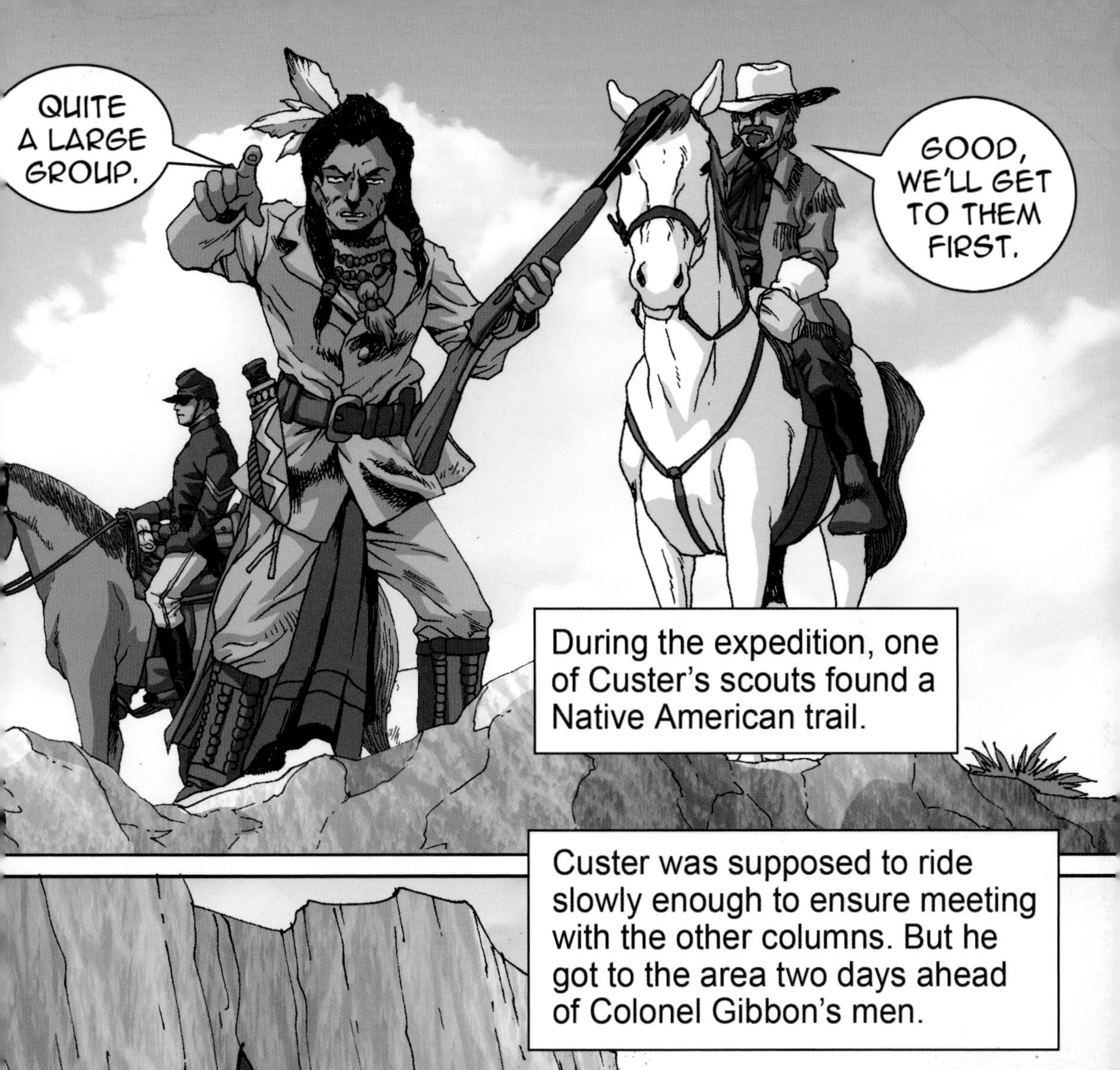
QUITE A LARGE GROUP.
GOOD, WE'LL GET TO THEM FIRST.
During the expedition, one of Custer's scouts found a Native American trail.

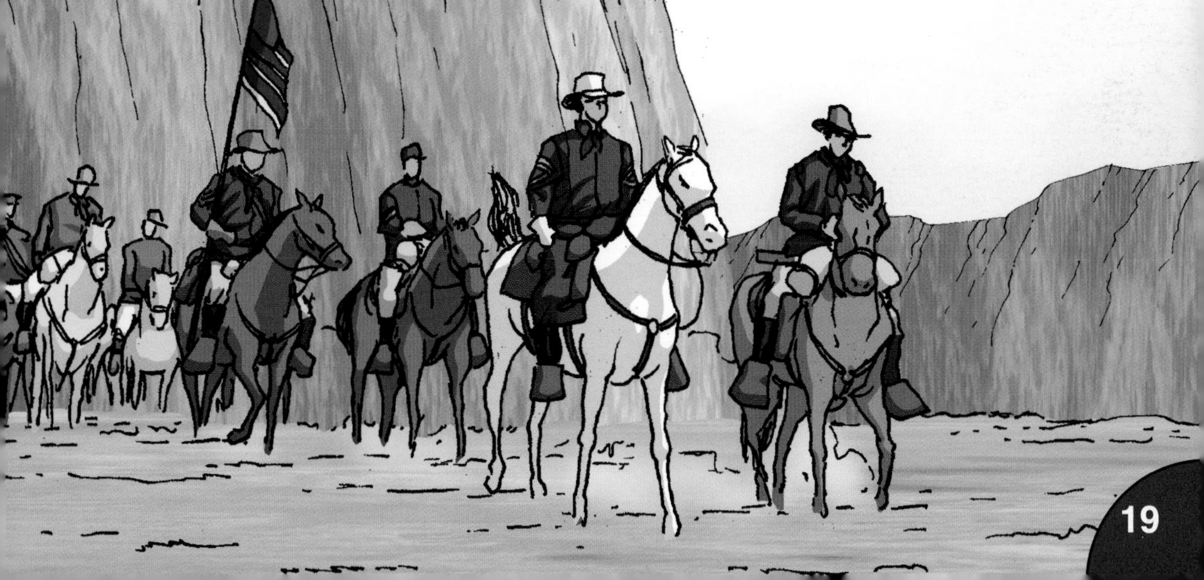
Custer was supposed to ride slowly enough to ensure meeting with the other columns. But he got to the area two days ahead of Colonel Gibbon's men.

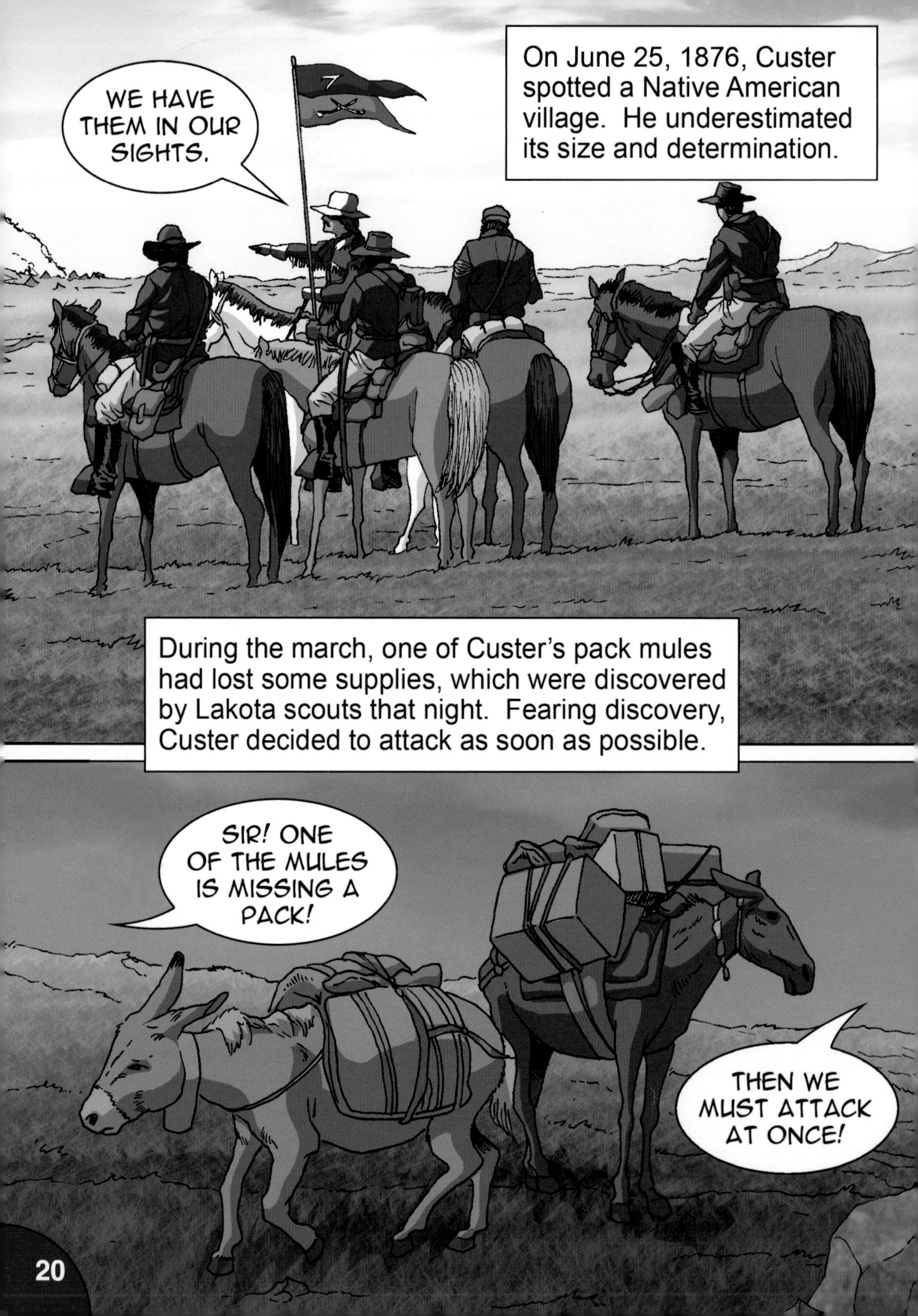
On June 25, 1876, Custer spotted a Native American village. He underestimated its size and determination.
WE HAVE THEM IN OUR SIGHTS.
During the march, one of Custer's pack mules had lost some supplies, which were discovered by Lakota scouts that night. Fearing discovery, Custer decided to attack as soon as possible.
SIR! ONE OF THE MULES IS MISSING A PACK!
THEN WE MUST ATTACK AT ONCE!

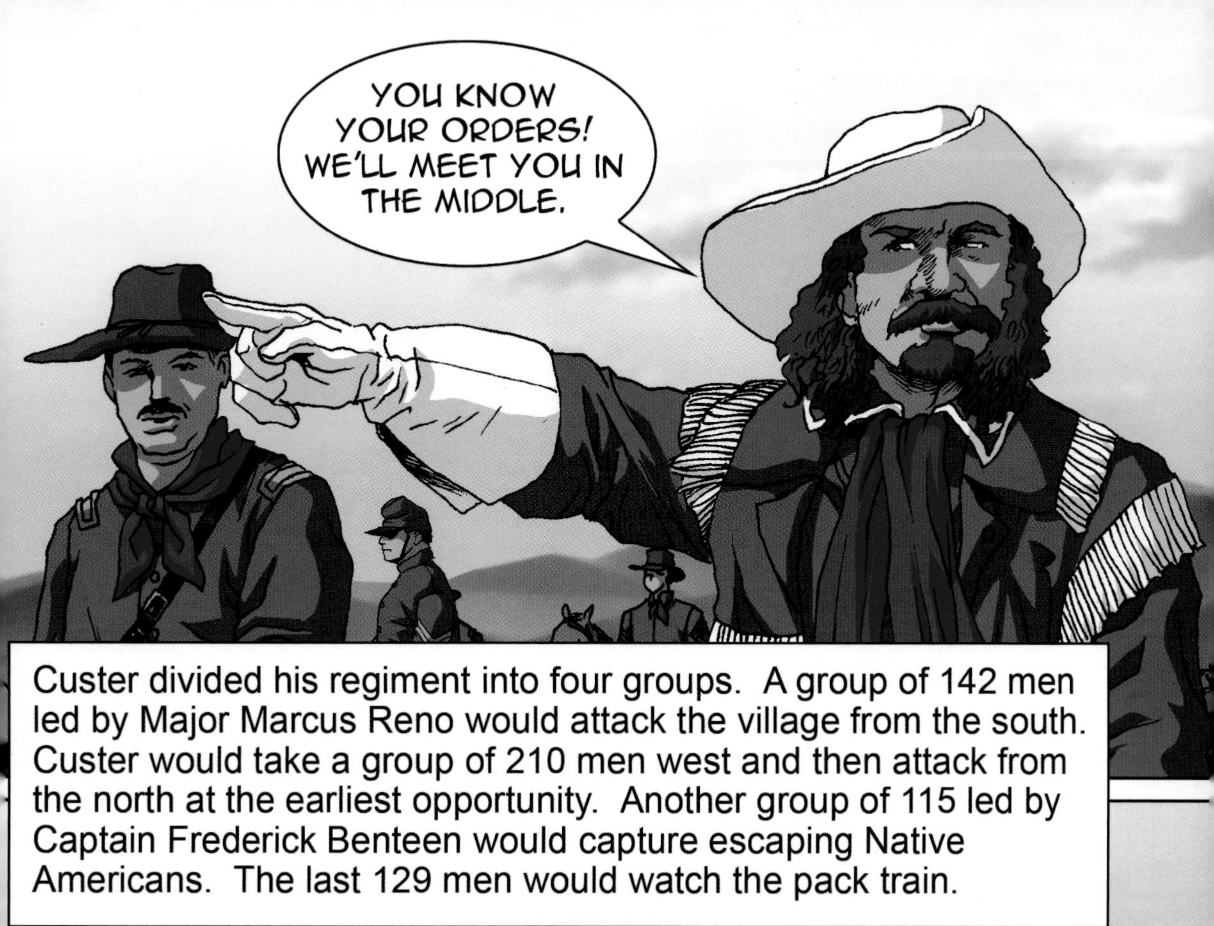
YOU KNOW YOUR ORDERS! WE'LL MEET YOU IN THE MIDDLE.
Custer divided his regiment into four groups. A group of 142 men led by Major Marcus Reno would attack the village from the south. Custer would take a group of 210 men west and then attack from the north at the earliest opportunity. Another group of 115 led by Captain Frederick Benteen would capture escaping Native Americans. The last 129 men would watch the pack train.

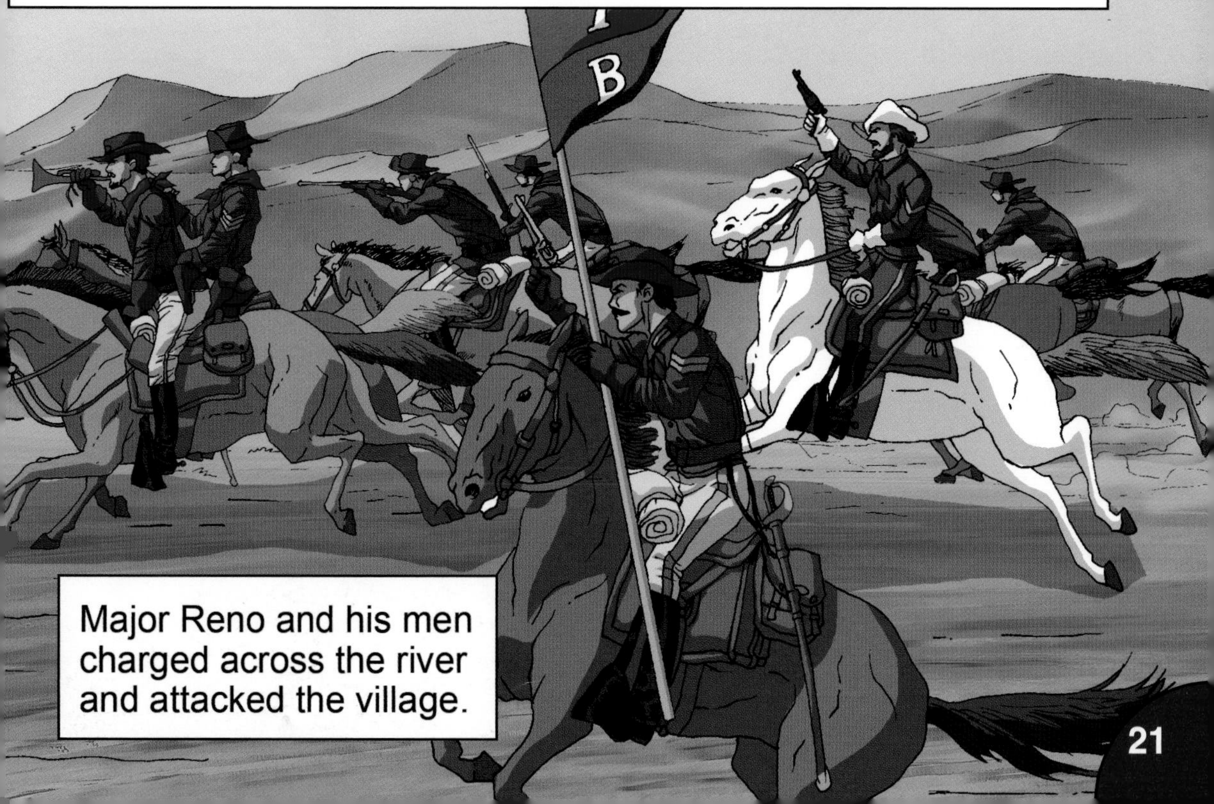
B
Major Reno and his men charged across the river and attacked the village.

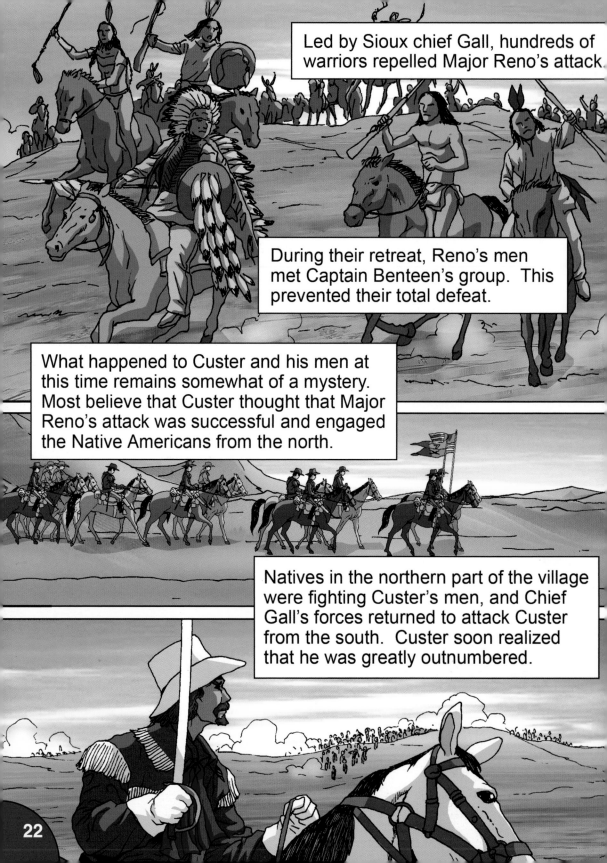

Led by Sioux chief Gall, hundreds of warriors repelled Major Reno's attack.

During their retreat, Reno's men met Captain Benteen's group. This prevented their total defeat.

What happened to Custer and his men at this time remains somewhat of a mystery. Most believe that Custer thought that Major Reno's attack was successful and engaged the Native Americans from the north.

Natives in the northern part of the village were fighting Custer's men, and Chief Gall's forces returned to attack Custer from the south. Custer soon realized that he was greatly outnumbered.

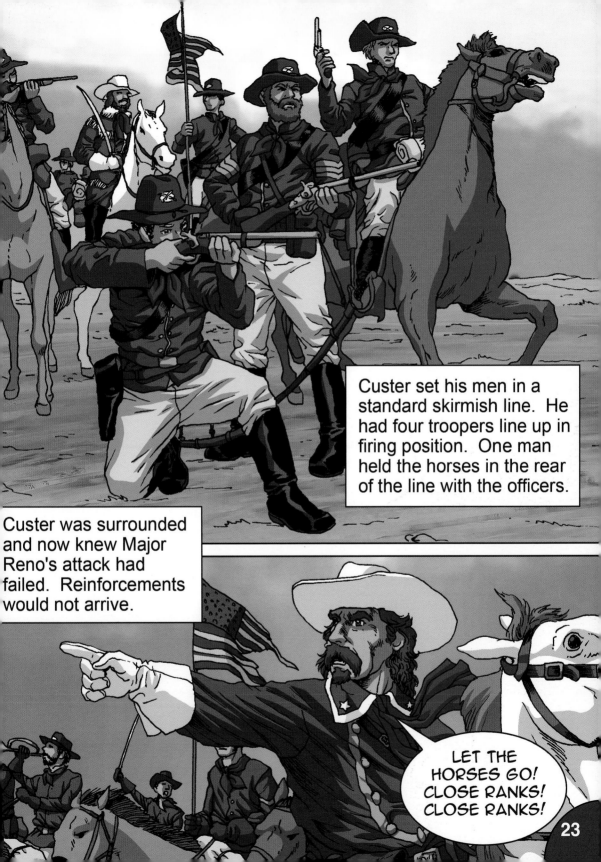

Custer set his men in a standard skirmish line. He had four troopers line up in firing position. One man held the horses in the rear of the line with the officers.

Custer was surrounded and now knew Major Reno's attack had failed. Reinforcements would not arrive.

LET THE HORSES GO! CLOSE RANKS! CLOSE RANKS!

Chapter 5 Custer's Last Stand

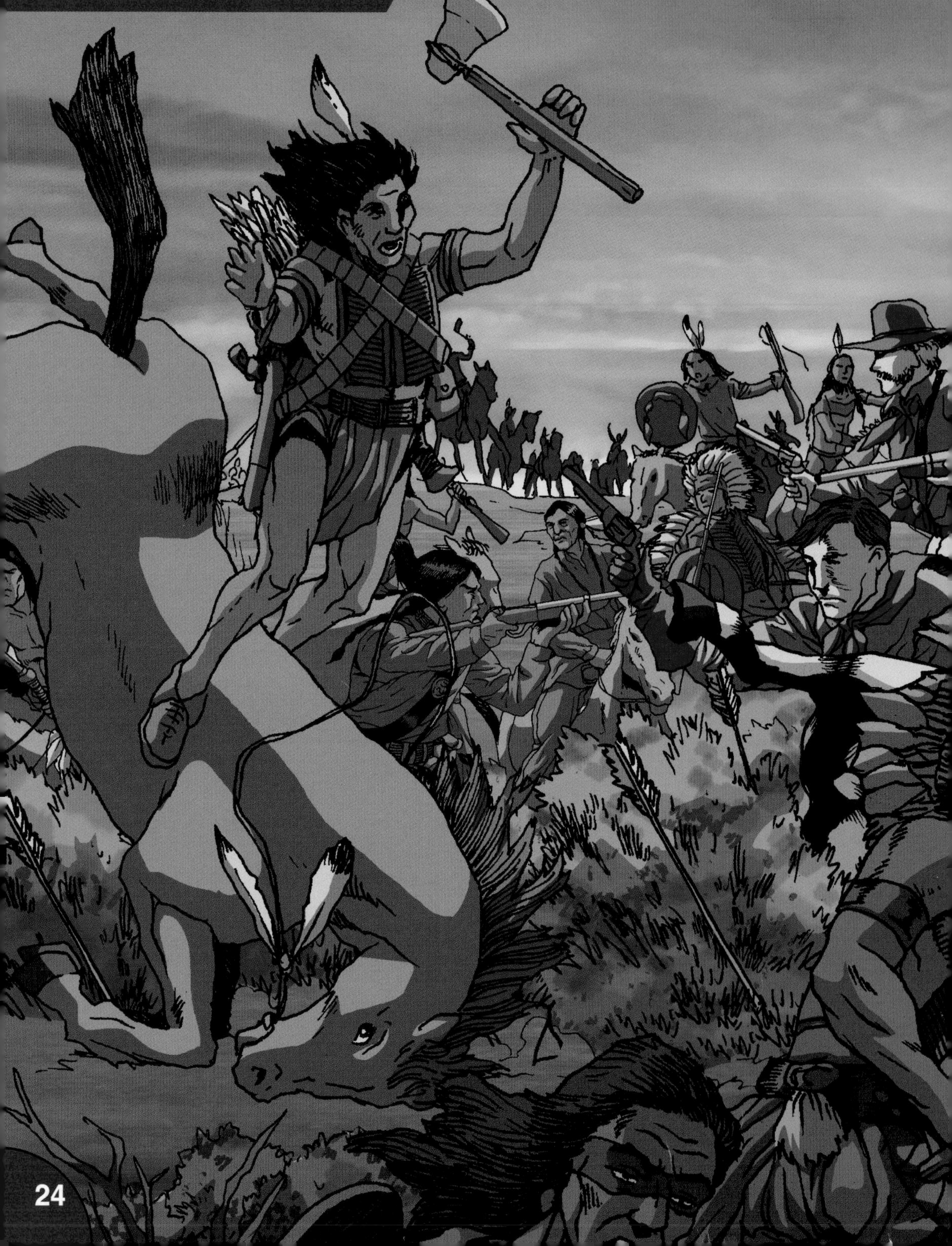

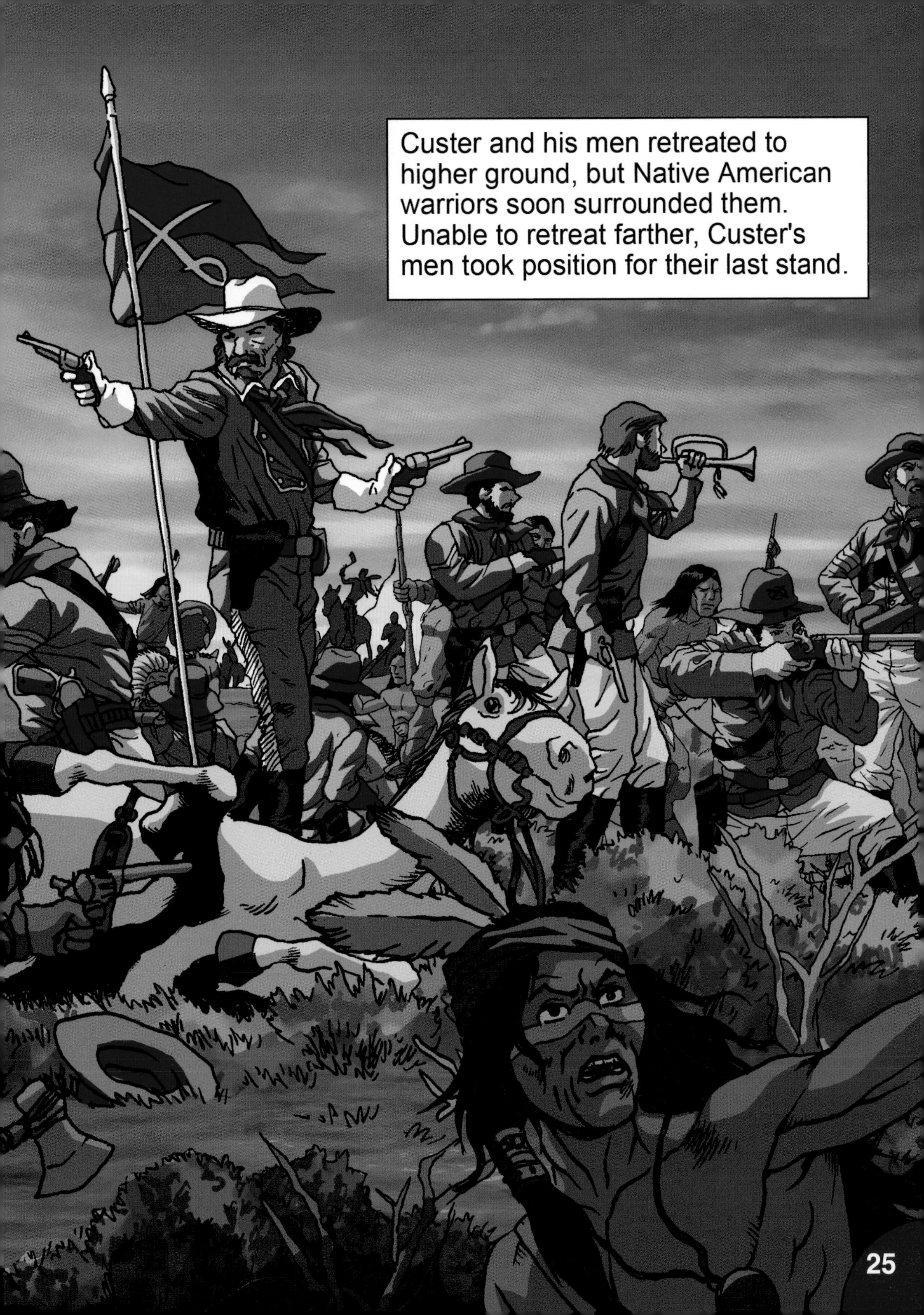
Custer and his men retreated to higher ground, but Native American warriors soon surrounded them. Unable to retreat farther, Custer's men took position for their last stand.

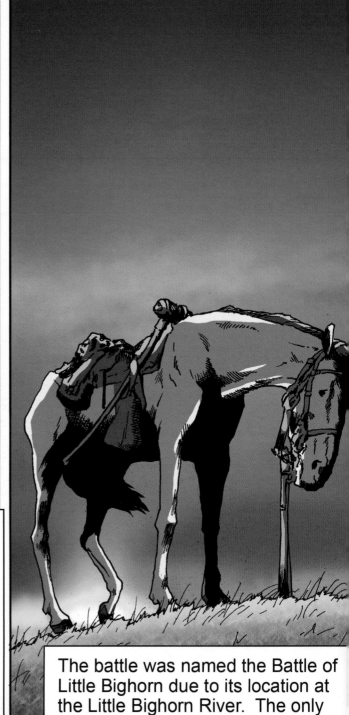

Due to the overwhelming odds, Custer and his men soon perished. The method of Custer's death remains controversial. Some believe he died in glorious battle, while others say he took his own life to avoid capture.

The battle was named the Battle of Little Bighorn due to its location at the Little Bighorn River. The only survivor is said to be a horse named Comanche.

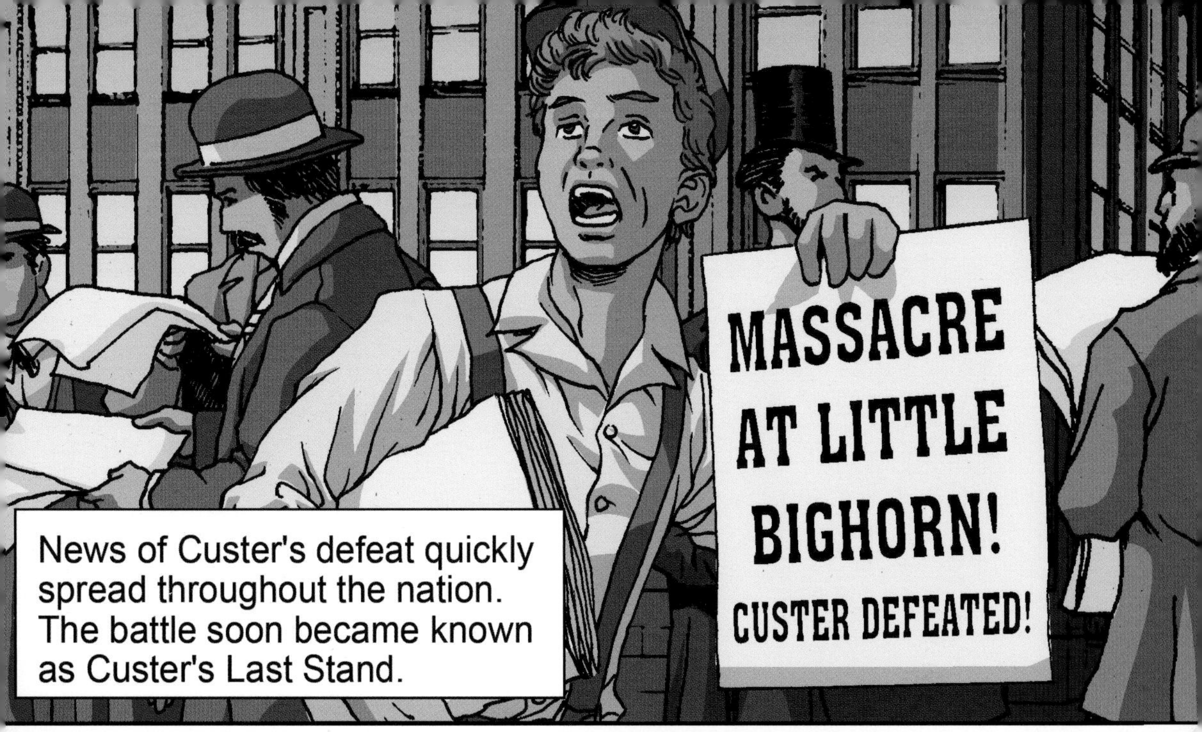
MASSACRE AT LITTLE BIGHORN!
CUSTER DEFEATED!
News of Custer's defeat quickly spread throughout the nation. The battle soon became known as Custer's Last Stand.

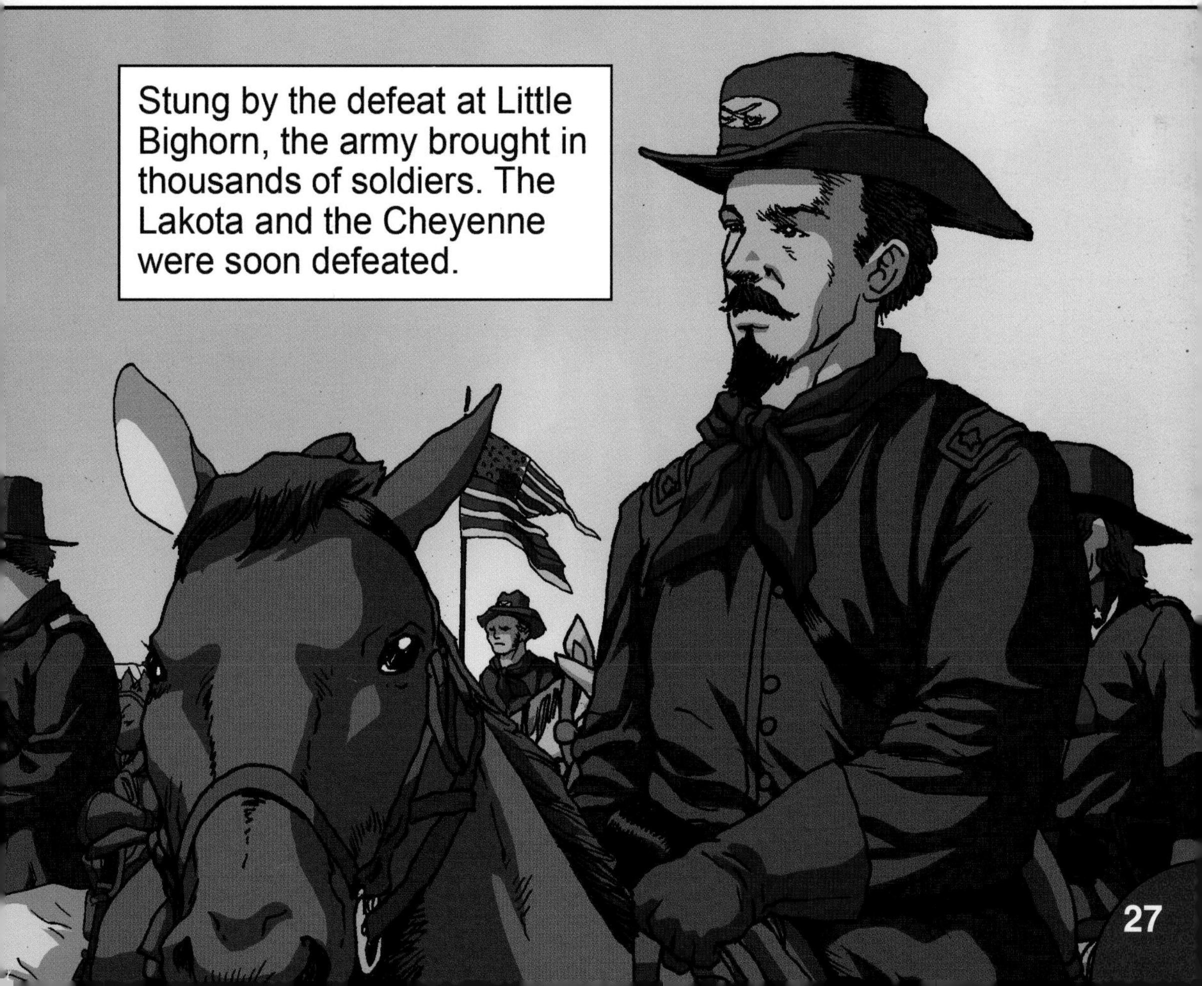
Stung by the defeat at Little Bighorn, the army brought in thousands of soldiers. The Lakota and the Cheyenne were soon defeated.

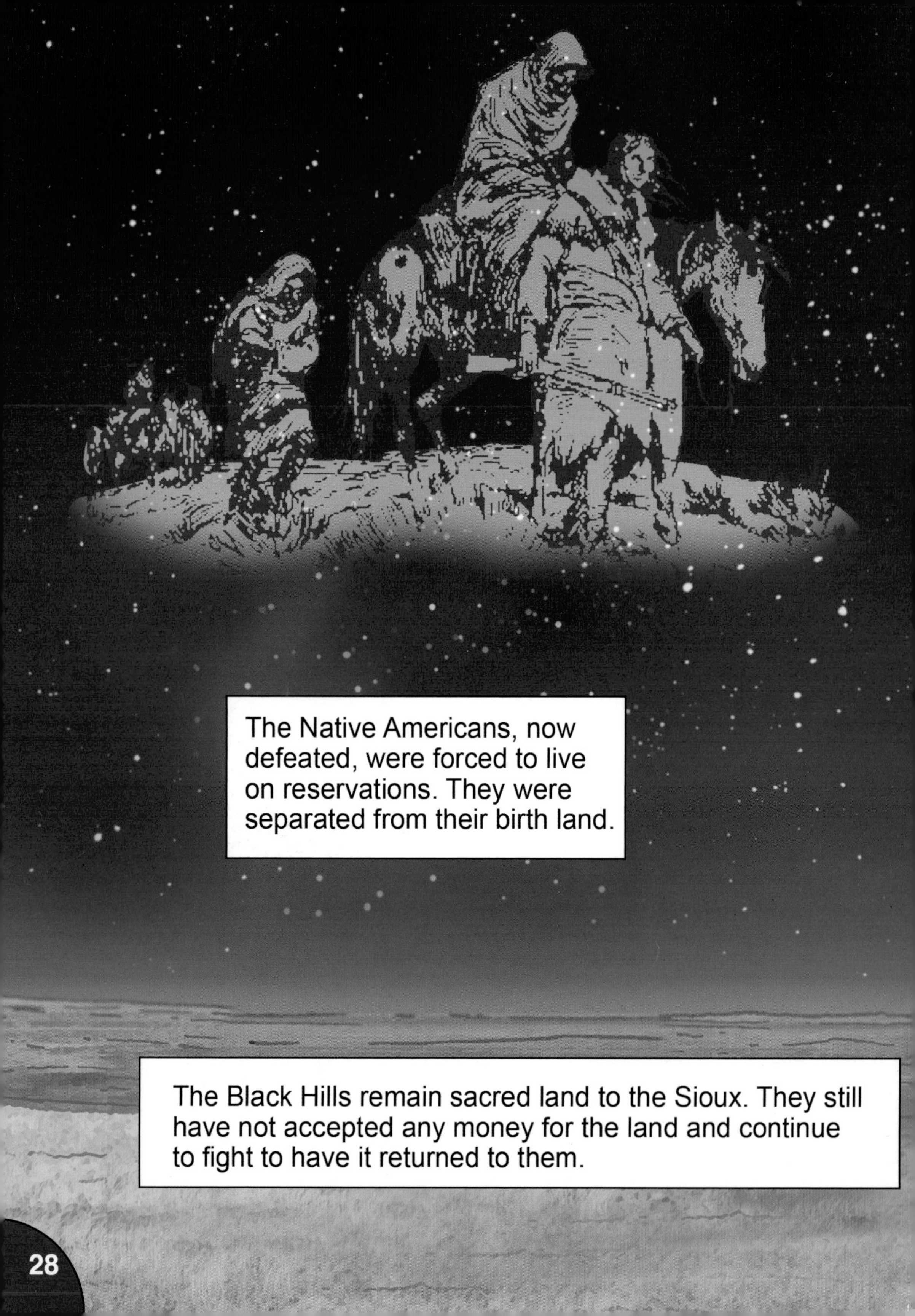
The Native Americans, now defeated, were forced to live on reservations. They were separated from their birth land.
The Black Hills remain sacred land to the Sioux. They still have not accepted any money for the land and continue to fight to have it returned to them.

The Custer National Cemetery contains the graves of Cavalrymen killed in Custer's Last Stand. Today, the last efforts of the Northern Plain Indians to stay on their sacred lands are remembered with a national monument in Montana.

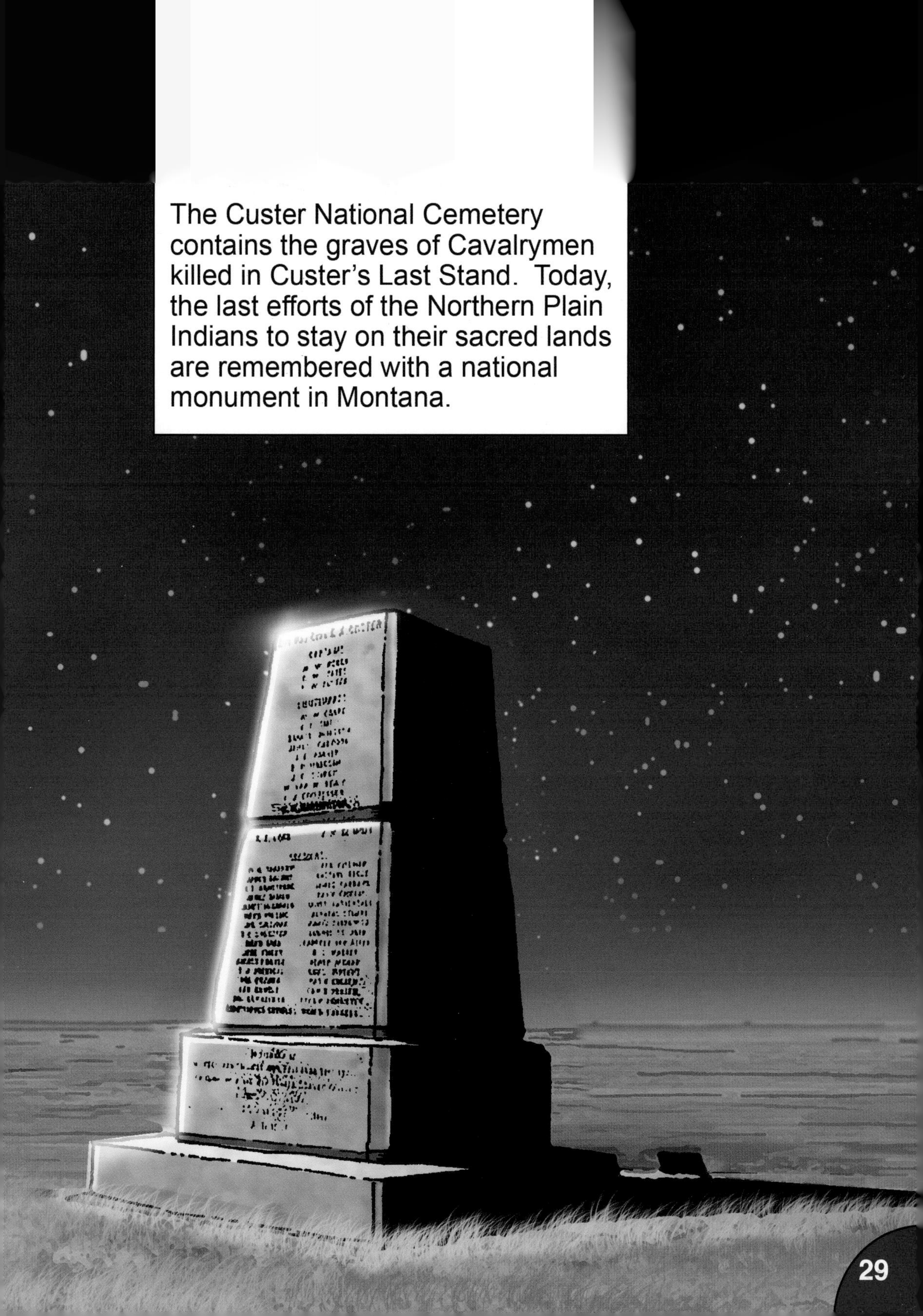

Map of Little Bighorn

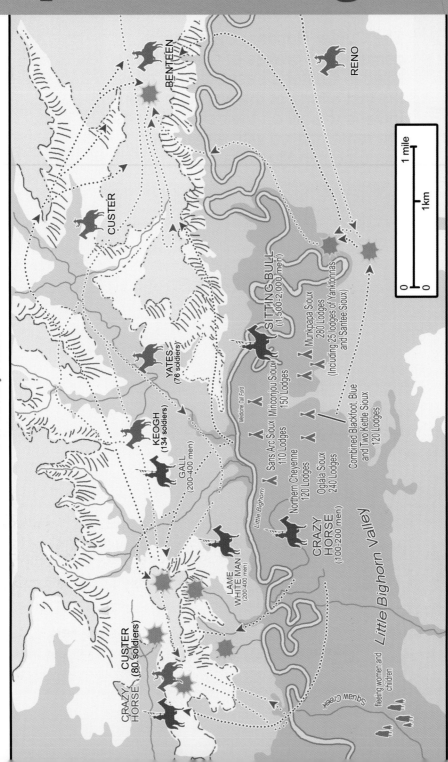

•••••••• Native American Route
•••••••• 7th Cavalry Route

RENO

BENTEEN

CUSTER

SITTING BULL
(1,500–2,000 men)

Munkpapa Sioux
280 Lodges
(Including 25 lodges of Yanktonnas
and Santee Sioux)

YATES
(76 soldiers)

Sans Arc Sioux
110 Lodges

Miniconjou Sioux
150 Lodges

Medicine Tail Ford

KEOGH
(134 soldiers)

GALL
(200–400 men)

Northern Cheyenne
120 Lodges

Oglala Sioux
240 Lodges

Combined Blackfoot, Blue
and Two Kettle Sioux
120 Lodges

Little Bighorn

CRAZY
HORSE
(100–200 men)

LAME
WHITE MAN
(200–400 men)

Little Bighorn Valley

CUSTER
(80 soldiers)

CRAZY
HORSE

fleeing women and
children

Squaw Creek

1 mile

1km

0

0

Glossary

civil war - a war between groups in the same country. The United States of America and the Confederate States of America fought a civil war from 1861 to 1865.

controversial - of or relating to something that causes discussion between groups with strongly different views.

Louisiana Purchase - land the United States purchased from France in 1803. It extended from the Mississippi River to the Rocky Mountains and from Canada to the Gulf of Mexico.

regiment - a military unit.

reinforcements - additional soldiers that are sent to strengthen an army.

reservation - a piece of land set aside by the government for Native Americans to live on.

Revolutionary War - from 1775 to 1783. A war for independence between Great Britain and its North American colonies. The colonists won and created the United States of America.

Web Sites

To learn more about Custer's Last Stand, visit ABDO Publishing Company on the World Wide Web at **www.abdopublishing.com**. Web sites about Custer's Last Stand are featured on our Book Links page. These links are routinely monitored and updated to provide the most current information available.

Index

B

Benteen, Frederick 21, 22

C

Chief Gall 22
Civil War 9, 12, 13
Clark, William 7, 8
Crazy Horse 10
Custer, George Armstrong 12,
    13, 18, 19, 20, 21, 22, 23, 25,
    26, 27

G

Gibbon, John 18, 19
government, U.S. 10, 11, 15

J

Jefferson, Thomas 6, 7

L

Lewis, Meriwether 7, 8
Louisiana Purchase 7

N

National Monument 29
Native Americans 8, 10, 11, 13
    14, 15, 16, 17, 18, 19, 20, 21,
    22, 25, 27, 28, 29

P

Paris, Treaty of 6

R

Reno, Marcus 21, 22, 23
reservations 10, 13, 28
Revolutionary War 6

S

Second Fort Laramie Treaty 11
    15
Sitting Bull 10

T

Terry, Alfred 18
transcontinental railroad 11, 12

Y

Yellowstone Expedition 12, 14